Problem Solving Study Guide

Mathematics
for
Elementary Teachers

A CONTEMPORARY APPROACH

Second Edition

Gary L. Musser
William F. Burger

OREGON STATE UNIVERSITY

Prepared by
Don Miller

ST. CLOUD STATE UNIVERSITY

D1379076

Macmillan Publishing Company

New York

Collier Macmillan Canada

Toronto

Maxwell Macmillan International

New York   Oxford   Singapore   Sydney

Copyright © 1991, Macmillan Publishing Company,
a division of Macmillan, Inc.

Printed in the United States of America

All rights reserved. No part of this book may be reproduced or
transmitted in any form or by any means, electronic or mechanical,
including photocopying, recording, or any information storage and
retrieval system, without permission in writing from the Publisher.

Macmillan Publishing Company
866 Third Avenue, New York, New York 10022

Collier Macmillan Canada, Inc.

Printing: 1 2 3 4 5 6 7   Year: 1 2 3 4 5 6 7

ISBN   0-02-381155-2

PREFACE

The purpose of this study guide is to provide preservice and inservice elementary and middle school teachers with non-routine problem solving experiences to help them become better problem solvers. Knowing when and how to apply a variety of strategies will, in turn, provide teachers with techniques that they can use in teaching problem solving in mathematics.

Each of the twenty-one sections in this study guide consists of four pages, which include the following components.

Strategy

Each section begins by introducing a strategy along with a problem to be analyzed by students individually or in small groups. The purpose of the opening problem is to introduce a particular strategy. Students should initially attempt to solve the problem by applying the given strategy even though an alternate strategy may, at times, seem more natural. Later, alternate approaches to solving problems will be encouraged. These initial pages have been designed to serve as overhead masters.

Solution

A solution to the opening problem is provided on the top of second page of each section. At first, these solutions are quite complete. However, as students progress through this study guide, they are asked to provide missing portions of the solutions. Also included are some questions related to the problem, a discussion of the strategy, and a list of clues suggesting when the strategy may be appropriate in solving a problem.

Practice Problems

The purpose here is to provide students with an opportunity to practice solving problems by applying this section's strategy.

Mixed Strategy Practice

Each section ends with a set of four problems that can be solved by using one or more of the strategies which have been introduced up to that point. After students have had ample time to analyze the problems, a discussion with students about their approaches should be very beneficial.

In addition to these sections, there are 84 additional practice problems. Answers for odd-numbered problems are found at the end of this study guide and answers to the even-numbered problems are contained in the Instructor's Manual for *Mathematics for Elementary Teachers - A Contemporary Approach* by Gary L. Musser and William F. Burger.

The problem solving strategies illustrated in this study guide are identical to those presented in the textbook *Mathematics for Elementary Teachers - A Contemporary Approach*. Thus, this study guide may be used in conjunction with the Musser/Burger textbook to provide students with additional non-routine problem solving experiences. In addition, this guide can serve to supplement any mathematics education course or workshop for elementary or middle school teachers where improving skills in problem solving is a main goal.

I wish to thank and commend Marilyn Wallace, Julie Borden, and Sue Borden for their expert word processing and Ron Bagwell for his creative artwork. I also wish to thank Gary Musser and Bill Burger for sharing their problem solving strategy clues with me for use in this study guide.

Don Miller

CONTENTS

1

Guess and Test

Tom and Barb have only nickels and dimes. Barb has 75 cents and Tom has 90 cents. Both have the same number of coins and Tom has the same number of dimes as Barb has nickels. How many nickels does Barb have?

SOLUTION

Problem: Tom and Barb have only nickels and dimes. Barb has 75 cents and Tom has 90 cents. Both have the same number of coins and Tom has the same number of dimes as Barb has nickels. How many nickels does Barb have?

Solution: Barb must have an odd number of nickels. Why? Barb and Tom have the same number of coins. The number of Barb's nickels equals the number of Tom's dimes.

	75¢ Barb			90¢ Tom		
	N	D		N	D	
Guess	⑨	3		0	⑨	$9 + 3 \neq 0 + 9$
Guess	⑤	5		8	⑤	$5 + 5 \neq 8 + 5$
⋮	⋮	⋮		⋮	⋮	
Guess	⑦	4		4	⑦	$7 + 4 = 4 + 7$

a.   This solution displays random guess and test. Describe a systematic way of solving it.
b.   Before solving the problem, it was noted that Barb must have an odd number of nickels. What conclusion can you draw about the number of nickels Tom has? Explain.
c.   Explain how the information like that in part b is helpful in solving the problem.

DISCUSSION

In using the Guess and Test strategy, the first step is to guess a possible answer to the question asked in the problem. A test is then made to determine if your guess satisfies the conditions of the problem. This process (guess and test) continues as you systematically try to improve your guesses until a solution is obtained.

CLUES

The Guess and Test strategy may be appropriate when:

*   There is a limited number of possible answers to test.
*   You want to gain a better understanding of the problem.
*   You have a good idea of what the answer is.
*   You can systematically try possible answers.
*   Your choices have been narrowed down by the use of other strategies.
*   There is no other obvious strategy to try.

PRACTICE PROBLEMS

Problem:	It costs 25 cents to mail a letter and 15 cents to mail a postcard. Tina wrote to 20 people last month. Her cost for postage was $4.40. How many postcards did she write during that time?

Solution: Guess and Test

	1st Guess	2nd Guess	3rd Guess	4th Guess
Number of letters	10	8	12	14
Number of postcards	10	12	8	6
Postage	$4.00	$3.80	$4.20	$4.40

Tina wrote 6 postcards and 14 letters.

1–A.   A rectangular field has a perimeter of 220 meters and an area of 2,856 square meters. What are its dimensions?

1–B.   The sum of two counting numbers is 91. Half of one number is three times the other number. What are the numbers?

4

MIXED STRATEGY PRACTICE

PROBLEM-SOLVING STRATEGIES

1. Guess and Test

1-1. The numbers 1 through 16 can be placed in a 4×4 array so that the sum of each row and the sum of the four corner numbers are the same. Find the missing numbers in the figure shown below.

15	*	*	4
*	3	*	5
8	*	*	11
1	12	*	*

1-2. Find the two counting numbers which have a difference of 21 and a product of 1,696.

1-3. Ken bought some pencils and erasers for $1.80. The erasers were 15 cents each and the pencils were 6 cents each. How many of each did he buy if he ended up with more erasers than pencils?

1-4. How can 7 trees be planted so that there are 6 rows of trees in a straight line with each row having 3 trees?

2

Use a Variable

After the first two terms in the following sequence, each number is the sum of the preceding two terms. Find the missing numbers.

4 ___ ___ ___ ___ 67

SOLUTION

Problem: After the first two terms in the following sequence, each number is the sum of the preceding two terms. Find the missing numbers.

4   __   __   __   __   67

Solution: Let x represent the second term of the sequence.

4   _____   _____   _____   _____   67
                          x $x + 4$ $2x + 4$ $3x + 8$ $5x + 12$

$$5x + 12 = 67 \longrightarrow x = 11$$

Check: 4   __11__   __15__   __26__   __41__   67
                       4 + 11   11 + 15   15 + 26   26 + 41

a.   This problem could have been solved using Guess and Test. Is the Use a Variable strategy preferable? Why or why not?

b.   What is it about this problem that suggests the Use a Variable strategy?

DISCUSSION

The Use a Variable strategy is often helpful when Guess and Test appears to be too inefficient. Also, there are times when a variable must be used. For example, consider the following products of consecutive even numbers increased by 1:

$$2 \times 4 + 1 = 9 = 3^2 \qquad 6 \times 8 + 1 = 49 = 7^2 \qquad 10 \times 12 + 1 = 121 = 11^2$$

These three examples suggest that a square will result in each such case. Since there are infinitely many even numbers, a variable must be employed.   Verify this conjecture for all possible even numbers as follows:

$$2N(2N + 2) + 1 = 4N^2 + 4N + 1 = (2N + 1)^2.$$

Thus, by using a variable, we have shown that this statement is true for all even numbers.

CLUES

The Use a Variable strategy may be appropriate when:

*   A phrase similar to "for any number" is present or implied.
*   A problem suggests an equation.
*   A proof or a general solution is required.
*   A problem contains phrases such as "consecutive", "even", "odd" , etc. whole numbers.
*   There is a large number of cases.
*   A proof is asked for in a problem involving numbers.
*   There is an unknown quantity related to known quantities.
*   There is an infinite number of numbers involved.
*   You are trying to develop a general formula.

PRACTICE PROBLEMS

Problem: The sum of two counting numbers is 91. Half of one number equals three times the other number. What are the numbers?

Solution: Use a Variable

Let x and y represent the two numbers.

The sum is 91: $x + y = 91$

Half of one equals 3 times the other: $\dfrac{x}{2} = 3y$ or $x = 6y$

$x + y = 91$ and $x = 6y$ implies that $6y + y = 91$

Hence, $y = 13$ and $x = 78$.

This problem was presented earlier in the Guess and Test section. The solution above shows a more efficient way to solve the problem.

2-A. Tom has 9 more baseball cards than Ken and Jill has 3 less than Randy. If Randy has 4 more cards than Ken, could the total numbers of cards they have be 45?

2-B. Show that any six consecutive even whole numbers can be written in the figure so that the sum of the three numbers on each side of the triangle is the same.

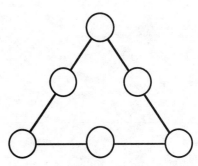

MIXED STRATEGY PRACTICE

PROBLEM-SOLVING STRATEGIES

1. Guess and Test
2. Use a Variable

2-1. Find the whole number represented by the fraction below without actually doing the calculations involved.

$$\frac{67897652^2 - 67897651 \times 67897653 + 67897650}{67897651}$$

2-2. Bruce was a pupil at Madison Elementary School in 1945. The year of his birth is a perfect square. How old was he on his birthday in 1988?

2-3. Write any three counting numbers in the first 3 blank spaces shown below. Continue with five more numbers, each being the sum of the preceding 3 terms. The sum of your eight numbers should be equal to 4 times the seventh number. Show why this must always be true.

___	___	___	___
1	2	3	4

___	___	___	___
5	6	7	8

2-4. In a group of cows and turkeys, the number of heads is 35 less than the number of legs. What is the largest number of cows that could be in this group of animals?

3 Look for a Pattern

How many beads are hidden under the cloud?

SOLUTION

Problem: How many beads are hidden under the cloud?

Solution: What patterns do the black beads and white beads make? What's hidden under the cloud; black beads, white beads, or some of both?

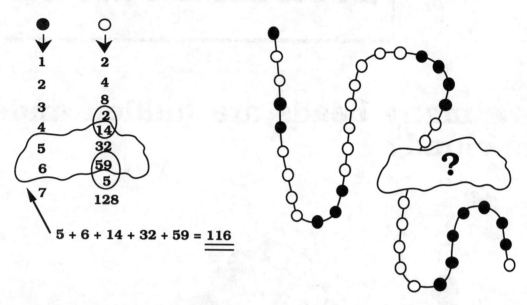

5 + 6 + 14 + 32 + 59 = <u>**116**</u>

a. Is Guess and Test appropriate for this problem? Why or why not?
b. Is the Use a Variable strategy helpful? Why or why not?

DISCUSSION

The Look for a Pattern strategy is often useful when a pattern is generated by systematically listing special cases of the problem. For many problems, the pattern leads directly to the answer, while others will require further insight before a solution can be realized.

CLUES

The Look for a Pattern strategy may be appropriate when:

*   A list of data is given.
*   A sequence or series of numbers is involved.
*   Listing special cases helps you deal with complex problems.
*   You are asked to make a prediction or generalization.
*   Information can be expressed and viewed in an organized manner, such as in a table.

PRACTICE PROBLEMS

Problem:	If the *s continue as shown below, what is the total number of *s that will be in sets R through T? A: ** B: **** C: ****** D: ******** E: ********** ...
Solution:	Look for a Pattern A → 2 *s B → 4 *s C → 6 *s D → 8 *s ... 1 2 3 4 5 6 18 19 20 A B C D E F ... R S T 2 4 6 8 10 12 ... 36 38 40 The total number of *s in R, S, and T is 114 (36 + 38 + 40).

3–A.   If the *s continue as shown below, how many *s will be in set T?

```
A  * * *              B  * * * *          C  * * * * * *      D  * * * * * * *
   * *                   * * * *             * * * * * *         * * * * * * *
                         * * * *             * * * * *           * * * * * * *
                                             * * * * *           * * * * * * *
                                             * * * * *           * * * * * * *
                                                                 * * * * * * *
                                                                 * * * * * * *
```

3–B.   <u>A</u> <u>1</u> <u>2</u> <u>3</u>   <u>B</u> <u>5</u> <u>6</u> <u>7</u>   <u>C</u> <u>9</u> <u>10</u> <u>11</u>   <u>D</u> <u>13</u> <u>14</u> <u>15</u>

Use the pattern suggested above to help you find the missing terms.

a) H ____ ____ ____   b) R ____ ____ ____

c) ____ ____ 50 ____   d) ____ ____ ____ 63

e) ____ ♣ ♥ ♠ where ♣ + ♥ + ♠ = 258.

12

MIXED STRATEGY PRACTICE

PROBLEM-SOLVING STRATEGIES

1. Guess and Test
2. Use a Variable
3. Look for a Pattern

3-1. Find the ones digit for each of the following. Ones digit:

3^1 ___ 3^2 ___ 3^3 ___ 3^4 ___

3^5 ___ 3^6 ___ 3^7 ___ 3^8 ___

Predict the ones digit:

a. 3^{41} _____   b. 3^{63} _____

c. 4^{99} _____   d. 7^{98} _____

3-2. Each girl in a seventh grade class has as many pencils as there are girls and each boy has as many pencils as there are boys. There are 30 students with a total of 468 pencils. How many girls are in the class if there are more girls than boys?

3-3. Red (R) and white (W) balls are placed into boxes labeled Box #1, Box #2, Box #3, and so on. The arrangement of balls in each box is as follows:

1R 3W	3R 6W	5R 11W
Box #1	Box #2	Box #3

7R 18W	9R 27W	11R 38W
Box #4	Box #5	Box #6

a. What is the total number of balls in box #29?
b. How many white balls are there in box #9?
c. What is the total number of red balls in the first 60 boxes?

3-4. Find the largest 5-digit perfect square that is divisible by 9.

4

Make a List

I am thinking of three different whole numbers which have a product of 36. Five more than the sum of the numbers is a perfect square. What is the sum of my numbers?

$1 \times 1 \times 36 = 36$

$1 \times 2 \times 18 = 36$

$1 \times 3 \times 12 = 36$

SOLUTION

Problem: I am thinking of three different whole numbers that have a product of 36. Five more than the sum of the numbers is a perfect square. What is the sum of my numbers?

Solution: The following list displays all possible triples of numbers whose product is 36.

A	B	C	A · B · C	A + B + C	A + B + C + 5
1	1	36	36	38	43
1	2	18	36	21	26
1	3	12	36	16	21
1	4	9	36	14	19
1	6	6	36	13	18
2	2	9	36	13	18
2	3	6	36	11	**16 = 4^2**
3	3	4	36	10	15

$$2 + 3 + 6 = \underline{\underline{11}}$$

a. Guess and Test could have been used to solve this problem. Is the Make a List strategy more efficient? Why or why not?
b. Why is Use a Variable not an efficient strategy for this problem?

DISCUSSION

An organized list sometimes leads directly to a solution or it may reveal a pattern that suggests a possible solution to the problem. For example, consider a list of all multiples of 99 between 1,000 and 2,000:

  1089   1188   1287   1386   1485   1584   1683   1782   1881   1980.

The list suggests that a 4-digit number A,BCD is a multiple of 99 when AB + CD = 99.

CLUES

The Make a List strategy may be appropriate when:

* Information can easily be organized and presented.
* Data can easily be generated.
* Listing the results obtained by using Guess and Test.
* Asked "In how many ways" something can be done.
* Trying to learn about a collection of numbers generated by a rule or formula.

PRACTICE PROBLEMS

Problem:	How many triangles of perimeter 12 inches are there if the length of each side must be a counting number?

Solution: Make a List

X:	1	1	1	1	1	2	2	2	2	3	3	4
Y:	1	2	3	4	5	2	3	4	5	3	4	4
Z:	10	9	8	7	6	8	7	6	5	6	5	4

The list contains all possible ways in which 12 can be written as the sum of 3 counting numbers. The lengths of the 3 sides, in inches, must be either 2, 5, and 5, 3, 4, and 5, or 4, 4, and 4. Why?

4–A.   Jill randomly tossed 3 darts at the board shown below. All hit the target. To win a prize, her total score must be either 66 or 75. Find all possible winning combinations.

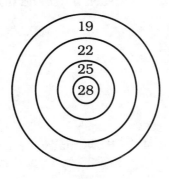

4–B.   Fred has a collection of dimes and quarters worth $2.50. Which of the following cannot be the total number of coins in his collection?

10   13   16   18   19   22   25

MIXED STRATEGY PRACTICE

PROBLEM-SOLVING
STRATEGIES

1. Guess and Test
2. Use a Variable
3. Look for a Pattern
4. Make a List

4–1.   1   1   2   3   5   8   13   21   ...

Use a pattern similar to the one shown above to help you fill in the missing numbers in each of the below sequences.

a.   1   2   __   __   __   __   21

b.   6   __   1   __   –3   __   –10

c.   2   __   __   0   __   __   2

d.   __   __   __   17   __   __   73

4–2. In how many ways can 3 girls divide 10 pennies if each must end up with at least one penny?

4–3. How many odd counting numbers less than 1,000 are not divisible by 7?

4–4. Is the sum of four consecutive counting numbers ever divisible by 4? If so, when? If not, why not?

5

Solve a Simpler Problem

3333333334^2 equals a 20-digit number. What is the sum of the digits?

SOLUTION

Problem: 3333333334^2 equals a 20-digit number. What is the sum of the digits?

Solution: Look at simpler related problems.

$$34^2 \qquad\qquad 334^2 \qquad\qquad 3334^2$$

$$1156 \qquad\qquad 111556 \qquad\qquad 11115556$$

Look for a pattern.

$$3333333334^2 = \underbrace{111...1}_{\text{Ten 1's}} \ \underbrace{555...5}_{\text{Nine 5's}} \ 6$$

Sum of the digits: $10 + 45 + 6 = \underline{\underline{61}}$

a. Why was the Solve a Simpler Problem strategy used in this problem?
b. The 3 and 4 involved in this problem are consecutive digits. Will any similar problem with consecutive digits result in a pattern?

DISCUSSION

The Solve a Simpler Problem strategy can be used in solving many complex problems by looking at simpler related cases. A list of the data generated provides further insight and often reveals a pattern that suggests a solution.

CLUES

The Solve a Simpler Problem strategy may be appropriate when:

* The problem involves complicated computations.
* The problem involves very large or very small numbers.
* You are asked to find the sum of a series of numbers.
* A direct solution is too complex.
* You want to gain a better understanding of the problem.
* The problem involves a large array or diagram.

PRACTICE PROBLEMS

Problem: In how many different ways can a dozen identical red chips be placed into three separate piles if each pile must end up with at least one chip?

Solution: Solve a Simpler Problem

3 chips: 1   1   1   (1 way)   4 chips: 1   1   2   1   2   1   2   1   1   (3 ways)

Show that 5 chips can be put into the piles 6 ways.

Number of chips	3	4	5	6	7	8	...	12
Number of ways	1	3	6	10	15	21		

The pattern suggests that the answer to the problem is 55. Verify.

5–A.   How many different rectangles are there in the figure shown at right?

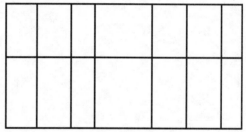

5–B.   A box contains a set of 864 chips. Each chip has either one dot 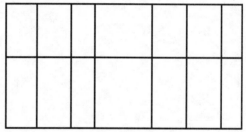, two dots , or no dots on one side. Most of the 864 chips have one dot and exactly half of the other chips have 2 dots. What is the total number of dots on all 864 chips?

MIXED STRATEGY PRACTICE

PROBLEM-SOLVING STRATEGIES

1. Guess and Test
2. Use a Variable
3. Look for a Pattern
4. Make a List
5. Solve a Simpler Problem

5-1. Thirteen identical rectangular cards are arranged as shown to form a large rectangle of perimeter 53 centimeters. What is the area of the large rectangle?

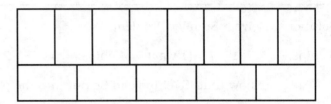

5-2. Find three perfect squares whose product is 45 less than the largest 4-digit perfect cube.

5-3. What is the average of the following pattern of numbers hidden under the cloud?

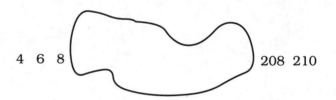

4 6 8   208 210

5-4. Row 1   1
      Row 2   3   5
      Row 3   7   9   11
      Row 4   13   15   17   19
      Row 5   21   23   25   27   29

   a. Find the middle number in the 99th row.
   b. What is the sum of the numbers in the 30th row?
   c. Find the difference between the first number in row 90 and the first number in row 89.

6

Draw a Picture

The surface of Big Lake is 31 feet above the surface of Long Lake. Long Lake is half as deep as Big Lake and the bottom of Long Lake is 8 feet below the bottom of Big Lake. How deep is each lake?

SOLUTION

Problem: The surface of Big Lake is 31 feet above the surface of Long Lake. Long Lake is half as deep as Big Lake and the bottom of Long Lake is 8 feet below the bottom of Big Lake. How deep is each lake?

Solution: Draw a Picture

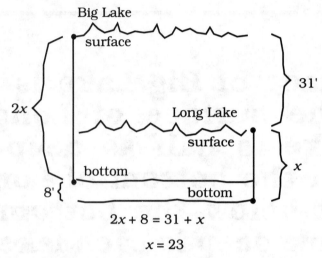

$$2x + 8 = 31 + x$$

$$x = 23$$

Big Lake is 46' deep and Long Lake is 23' deep.

a.   Convince yourself that the Draw a Picture strategy is helpful by trying to solve the problem without a picture.
b.   What is the depth of Clear Lake given that its surface is 10 feet below the surface of Big Lake and its bottom is 6 feet above the bottom of Long Lake?

DISCUSSION

Many problems involve physical situations where the Draw a Picture strategy is helpful. A picture provides a visual representation that usually leads to a better understanding of the problem. This, in turn, often helps in devising a plan.

CLUES

The Draw a Picture strategy may be appropriate when:

*   A physical situation is involved.
*   Geometric figures or measurements are involved.
*   You want to gain a better understanding of the problem.
*   A visual representation of the problem is possible.

PRACTICE PROBLEMS

Problem: A club has twenty rectangular tables that seat 3 people along each side and one person on each end. These tables were placed end-to-end to form a long rectangular table. How many people can be seated in this arrangement? In general, how many people can be seated around n tables arranged in this way?

Solution: Draw a Picture.

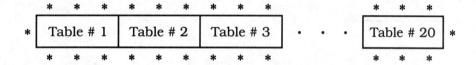

Sixty (3×20) people can be seated along each side, one on each end.

Hence, 122 people can be seated at the long table. $(2 \times 60 + 2 \times 1 = 122)$

In general, $6n + 2$ people can be seated around n tables.

6–A.   A "Superbounce" ball rebounds half the height it drops. The ball is dropped from a height of 176 feet. How far off the ground is the ball when it has traveled a total of 500 feet?

6–B.   An office building has 33 floors, each 10 feet high, and elevators that travel at a constant speed. If it takes 10 seconds for an elevator to go from the first floor to the fifth floor, how long will it take an elevator to go from the fifth floor to the middle floor?

MIXED STRATEGY PRACTICE

PROBLEM-SOLVING STRATEGIES

1. Guess and Test
2. Use a Variable
3. Look for a Pattern
4. Make a List
5. Solve a Simpler Problem
6. Draw a Picture

6–1. On a certain 20 question test, a student receives 4 points for each correct answer, loses 3 points for each incorrect answer, and loses 2 points if no answer is given. Todd took the test and scored 34 points. How many problems did he answer correctly?

6–2. Fencing is sold in 8 foot sections at $15 per section. Fence posts cost $4 each. How much will it cost to build a fence around a square field which is 240 feet on each side?

6–3. Each of three boxes X, Y, and Z contains at least 4 marbles. The total number of marbles is 36. There are twice as many marbles in box X as in box Y and box Z contains an odd number of marbles. What is the smallest number of marbles that could be in box Z?

6–4. Each day, Jason walks to his office at a constant rate. One-third of the way he passes a bank and three–fourths of the way to work he passes a store. At the bank his watch reads 6:52 A.M. and at the store it reads 7:02 A.M. At what time was Jason halfway to his office?

7

Draw a Diagram

Lake City Jr. High Students

* 12 out of every 18 ride a bus to school.
* 9 out of every 15 live in Lake City.
* 160 ride a bus to school.

How many of the Jr. High students do not live in Lake City?

SOLUTION

Problem: Lake City Jr. High Students

* 12 out of every 18 ride a bus to school.
* 9 out of every 15 live in Lake City.
* 160 ride a bus to school.

How many of the Jr. High students do not live in Lake City?

Solution: Ride the bus: 12 out of 18, or 2 out of 3
Live in Lake City: 9 out of 15, or 3 out of 5

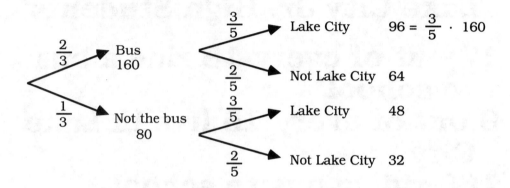

96 students do not live in Lake City

a.   A tree diagram was used to help solve this problem. Is a Venn diagram also useful in solving the problem? Why or why not?
b.   The solution shows that 80 students do not ride the bus. Explain why 48 of those students must live in Lake City.

DISCUSSION

The Draw a Diagram strategy can often be used to systematically represent the details in a problem. For example, the tree diagram to the right shows all 3-digit numbers less than 300 that contain only the digits 2, 3, 5, and 6 if each digit must be different.

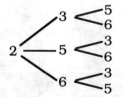

CLUES

The Draw a Diagram strategy may be appropriate when:

* The problem involves sets, prime factorization, ratios, or probabilities.
* An actual picture can be drawn, but a diagram is more efficient.
* Representing relationships among quantities.

PRACTICE PROBLEMS

Problem: In a group of 37 people, 18 are neither overweight nor lawyers. Ten are overweight and 13 are lawyers. How many lawyers in the group are not overweight?

Solution: Draw a Diagram

10 are overweight   13 are lawyers

18 are neither overweight nor lawyers implies that 19 are either overweight or lawyers. Why?

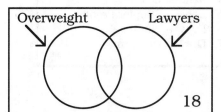

Hence, 4 are overweight lawyers. Why?

Therefore, 9 lawyers are not overweight? Why?

7–A.   If all of the digits must be different, how many 3-digit odd numbers greater than 700 can be written using only the digits 1, 2, 3, 5, 6, and 7?

7–B.   Of the 36 cars in a parking lot, 6 are red compact cars, 5 are red 2-door cars, and 7 are 2-door compacts. Half are not red, 13 are compacts, 20 have 4 doors, and 2 of the compact 4-door cars are not red. How many of the red 4-door cars in the parking lot are not compacts?

MIXED STRATEGY PRACTICE

PROBLEM-SOLVING STRATEGIES

1. Guess and Test
2. Use a Variable
3. Look for a Pattern
4. Make a List
5. Solve a Simpler Problem
6. Draw a Picture
7. Draw a Diagram

7-1. Two men, each weighing 200 pounds, and their two sons weighing 100 pounds each, crossed a river in a small boat that can carry only 200 pounds. How did they manage to cross the river?

7-2. In how many different ways can Ted, Amy and Bart divide 9 nickels if each gets at least one nickel and each must end up with a different amount of money?

7-3. A computer company has 11 sales offices. Each office is to be connected to all the other offices by a direct telephone line. How many telephone lines will be needed to complete the job?

7-4. A scout troop took in $800 selling T-shirts and caps at the County Fair. They sold 200 T-shirts and 60 caps. How many youth T-shirts did they sell based on the following unit prices?

Adult T's:	$4.00
Youth T's:	$3.00
Caps:	$2.00

8

Use Direct Reasoning

Each chip in two of the piles shown above weighs 8 grams. Each chip in the other pile weighs 7 grams. Show how to determine the pile that contains the 7-gram chips with only one weighing on a postal scale (not a balance scale).

SOLUTION

Problem:

Each chip in two of the piles shown above weighs 8 grams. Each chip in the other pile weighs 7 grams. Show how to determine the pile that contains the 7-gram chips with only one weighing on a postal scale (not a balance scale).

Solution: Take 1 chip from pile A, 2 from B, and 3 from C.

Total weight = 47 g.	A has the 7-gram chips
Total weight = 46 g.	B has the 7-gram chips
Total weight = 45 g.	C has the 7-gram chips

a. Are these the only possible total weights that may be obtained by choosing six chips in this manner? Explain.

b. Could this problem have been solved by placing all the chips on a scale? Why or why not?

DISCUSSION

Most problems involve the use of the Direct Reasoning strategy in conjunction with other strategies. Problems where direct reasoning is useful are often of the form "If $A_1, A_2, A_3, ...,$ then B" where a conclusion B holds true when a series of one or more given conditions also hold true. For example, the problem "If x, y, and z are odd, then $x + 2y + 3z$ is even" is solved directly by first assuming that x, y, and z are odd, and then observing that x and $3z$ are odd and $2y$ is even. Hence, $x + 2y + 3z$ must be even.

CLUES

The Use Direct Reasoning Strategy may be appropriate when:

*   A proof is required.
*   A statement of the form "If ..., then..." is involved.
*   You see a statement that you want to imply from a collection of known conditions.

PRACTICE PROBLEMS

Problem: There are 24 coins and a balance scale. The coins are alike in every way except that one of them is counterfeit and slightly heavier than the other 23 coins. What is the least number of weighings needed on the balance scale to determine the heavier coin?

Solution: Use Direct Reasoning

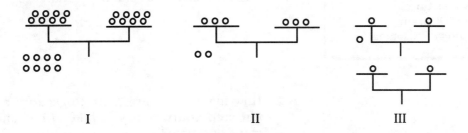

I   II   III

The figures shown above represent a solution to the problem. Why? Could the counterfeit coin be determined in 3 weighings when the total number of coins is 25? 26? 27? 28?

8–A.   Use the given clues to find the number represented by each letter.

* All are different one-digit whole numbers.
* The 4 corner numbers are all even.
* F is less than C and C × F = 0.
* ABC is a 3–digit number divisible by 9.
* D is a prime number.
* A + D = 10 and B + E = 13.
* E is one more than the average of A, B, and C.

A	B	C
D	E	F

8–B.   There are two boxes. One contains $100 and the other contains one penny. There are also two computers. One always tells the truth about the boxes and the other one never tells the truth. You don't know which box contains $100, nor which computer always tells the truth. You are allowed to ask one question of one computer. What question should you ask to be sure of selecting the box that contains $100?

MIXED STRATEGY PRACTICE

**PROBLEM-SOLVING
STRATEGIES**

1. Guess and Test
2. Use a Variable
3. Look for a Pattern
4. Make a List
5. Solve a Simpler Problem
6. Draw a Picture
7. Draw a Diagram
8. Use Direct Reasoning

8-1. Two baseball teams, A and B, played a double header. Use the clues given below to find all possible scores for the two games.

* Team A won the 1st game by 3 runs.
* Team B won the 2nd game by 1 run.
* Team A scored a total of 11 runs.
* Team B scored a total of 9 runs.

8-2. How many ways are there to get to the top of a ten step stairway if you take either one or two steps at a time?

8-3. After being warned about the dangers of smoking, a man decided to cut back 2 cigarettes a day. Keeping his promise, he continued cutting back 2 per day for one week. He smoked 91 cigarettes during the week. How many did he smoke the day before he started to cut back?

8-4. A computer was used to find the sum of the first 22 terms in the sequence of numbers whose first six terms are shown below. What digit is in the thousands place of the sum?

7, 77, 777, 7777, 77777, 777777, . . .

9

Use Indirect Reasoning

Show how 2 nickels, 4 dimes, and 3 quarters can be placed into a 3 by 3 array so that each row and column contains a different amount of money.

SOLUTION

Problem: Show how 2 nickels, 4 dimes, and 3 quarters can be placed into a 3 by 3 array so that each row and column contains a different amount of money.

Solution: First show why the coins in the 4 corners cannot all be dimes.

D	X	D
Y		Z
D	W	D

Suppose there is a dime in each corner. Then X, Y, Z, and W must be coins of different denominations. (Impossible.) Why? Therefore, the 4 coins in the corners cannot all be dimes.

Then show why the 3 quarters cannot all be in the same row or column.

Q	Q	Q
W	X	D
Y	Z	D

Suppose all the quarters are in the top row. This means that there must be 2 dimes in the same column. Why? Two dimes and 2 nickels remain. Hence, there is no solution. Why? Therefore, the 3 quarters cannot all be in the top row.

Solve the problem.

D	Q	D	45
D	Q	Q	60
D	N	N	20
30	55	40	

a. Does the discussion in the second part above guarantee that the 3 quarters cannot be in the same row or column?
b. Why is Indirect Reasoning useful in solving this problem?

DISCUSSION

The Use Indirect Reasoning strategy is helpful when a direct solution is either too complex or impossible. For example, suppose you are asked to prove that every odd counting number that is a perfect square is the square of an odd number. Looking directly at several examples such as 25, 49, and 81 suggests that the statement is true. However, this does not prove that it is always true. In using indirect reasoning, we start by assuming that the number is even $(2n)$, after which it can easily be shown that its square, $4n^2$, is also even. Hence, we can conclude that the number must be odd.

CLUES

The Use Indirect Reasoning strategy may be appropriate when:

*   Direct Reasoning seems too complex or does not lead to a solution.
*   Assuming the negation of what you are trying to prove narrows the scope of the problem.
*   A proof is required.

PRACTICE PROBLEMS

Problem:	Three burglars were caught breaking into a store. When questioned by the police, at least one of the 3 told the truth and at least one of the 3 lied. The statements made were as follows: Bob: It was Ken's idea. Ken: That's right, it was my idea. Barb: It wasn't my idea. Show why it could not have been Barb's idea to rob the store.
Solution:	Use Indirect Reasoning Suppose it was Barb's idea to rob the store. Therefore, Bob lied. We can now conclude that Ken lied. This means that all three lied. Why? This is impossible since at least one of the three told the truth. Hence, it was not Barb's idea.

9–A.   Five consecutive whole numbers whose sum is odd satisfy the following condition: $A + C + E = B + C + D$. Show why C cannot be even.

9–B.   Suppose you know that one of the statements on the cards represented below is true and the other is false. Show why the triangle cannot be on the back side of card A.

This card has a triangle drawn on the back side and the other card has a circle on the back	One of these cards has a triangle drawn on the back side and one of the cards has a circle on the back.
Card A	Card B

MIXED STRATEGY PRACTICE

PROBLEM-SOLVING
STRATEGIES

1. Guess and Test
2. Use a Variable
3. Look for a Pattern
4. Make a List
5. Solve a Simpler Problem
6. Draw a Picture
7. Draw a Diagram
8. Use Direct Reasoning
9. Use Indirect Reasoning

9–1. A farmer constructed a fence around a square field which is 400 meters on each side. He then divided the field into four equal areas by constructing fences across the middle vertically and horizontally. If all of the posts in the fence are 8 meters apart, how many posts did he use?

9–2. What is the remainder when 5^{99} is divided by:

a. 2? b. 3? c. 7?

9–3. Kennedy won the city track meet with 84 points. Lincoln scored twice as many points as Jefferson and Madison scored half as many points as Jefferson. Altogether, the total for two of the four teams was 95 and the total number of points scored by all teams was greater than 200. How many points did Lincoln score in the track meet?

9–4. During my vacation last summer it rained on 13 days. But when it rained in the morning, the afternoon was dry. Also, every rainy afternoon was preceded by a dry morning. There were 11 dry mornings and 12 dry afternoons. How many days long was my vacation?

10

Use Properties of Numbers

The owner of the Pizza Palace purchased 3 dozen caps for the softball teams he sponsors. He wanted to keep the price below $10 per cap. If one of the following represents the total cost, what was the cost per cap? Here, A, B, and C represent the hundreds digits.

$A06.40 $B51.24 $C39.68

you lika de hats?

SOLUTION

Problem: The owner of the Pizza Palace purchased 3 dozen caps for the softball teams he sponsors. He wanted to keep the price below $10 per cap. If one of the following represents the total cost, what was the cost per cap? Here, A, B, and C represent the hundreds digits.

$A06.40 $B51.24 $C39.68

Solution: The total cost must be divisible by 4 and 9. Why?
            All given totals are divisible by 4. Why?

9 divides $A06.40 only when A = 8
9 divides $B51.24 only when B = 6
9 divides $C39.68 only when C = 1

$806.40 ÷ 36 = $22.40 $139.68 ÷ 36 = $3.88 $651.24 ÷ 36 = $18.09

Thus, the cost for each cap was $3.88.

a.   Why is there only one possible value for each of A, B, and C?
b.   Would Guess and Test be an efficient way to solve the problem?

DISCUSSION

An understanding of properties of numbers often provides a more efficient way to solve a problem involving whole numbers. For example, knowing the divisibility tests for 4 and 9 allows one to quickly conclude that the number 4,000,000,032 is divisible by 36 even though you might not be able to do this problem on your calculator.

CLUES

The Use Properties of Numbers strategy may be appropriate when:

*   Special types of numbers such as odds, evens, primes, etc. are involved.
*   A problem can be simplified by using certain properties.
*   A problem involves lots of computation.

PRACTICE PROBLEMS ≡≡≡≡≡

Problem: Show why the numbers *M* and *N* shown below cannot be prime.

$$M = 19^7 + 7^{19} \times (13^7 - 7^{13}) + 3^5$$

$$N = 17! + 253 \quad (\text{Note:} \quad 17! = 17 \times 16 \times 15 \times \cdots \times 3 \times 2 \times 1)$$

Solution: Use Properties of Numbers

19^7, 7^{19}, $(13^7$, 7^{13}, and 3^5 must all be odd numbers. Why?
M = odd + odd × even + odd = even. Why?
Hence, M cannot be a prime number. Why?

17! and 253 are both divisible by 11. Why?
Therefore, 11 divides N = (17! + 253).
Hence, N cannot be a prime number.

10–A.   Find my 3-digit house number with the help of the following clues.

*   If you add 1 to the number, it is a multiple of 8.
*   If you add 5 to the number, it is a multiple of 9.
*   If you add 2 to the number, it is a multiple of 11.

10–B.   I am a 4-digit number with no repeating digits. I am divisible by 5, my first two digits (left to right) make a number divisible by 3, and my first three digits make a number divisible by 4. Also, my digits have a sum of 19 and I have the digit 7 in the thousands place. Who am I?

MIXED STRATEGY PRACTICE

PROBLEM-SOLVING
STRATEGIES

1. Guess and Test
2. Use a Variable
3. Look for a Pattern
4. Make a List
5. Solve a Simpler Problem
6. Draw a Picture
7. Draw a Diagram
8. Use Direct Reasoning
9. Use Indirect Reasoning
10. Use Properties of Numbers

10–1. Jim decided to put his collection of rare coins into a set of cups that are lined up on the kitchen table. Trying to put 5 coins into each cup, he ended up with only 2 coins in the last cup. When he put 3 coins into each cup, he had 9 coins left over. There are less than ten cups on the table. How many rare coins does Jim have?

10–2. How many different triangles are there in the given figure?

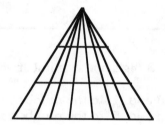

10–3. Karen and Beth bought identical boxes of stationery. Beth used hers to write one sheet letters and Karen used hers to write two sheet letters. Beth used all her envelopes and had 16 sheets left over. Karen used all her sheets and had 7 envelopes left over. How many envelopes were there in each box?

10–4. Mr. Leung builds ring-toss games with 1, 3 or 4 pegs. One day, he used 51 pegs to build 20 games. Find at least two different ways in which this can be done.

11

Solve an Equivalent Problem

At Tommie's yogurt shop you can order either a plain vanilla yogurt or you can order it with one or more of 6 toppings. How many different types of yogurt dishes can be ordered?

Now for your choice of toppings...

Tommie's Yogurt   Tasty!!

6 Delicious Toppings

Ron Bagwell ©

SOLUTION

Problem: At Tommie's yogurt shop you can order either a plain vanilla yogurt or you can order it with one or more of 6 toppings. How many different types of yogurt dishes can be ordered?

Solution: An equivalent problem is to determine the number of sets that are subsets of the 6–element set {A, B, C, D, E, F}. Why? The empty set represents a plain yogurt. By looking at simpler cases we can easily show that {A} has 2 subsets, {A, B} has 4 subsets, and {A, B, C} has 8 subsets. Extending this pattern suggests that the set {A, B, C, D, E, F} has 64 subsets. Hence, there are 64 ways to order a yogurt at Tommie's Yogurt Shop.

a.   How many ways can a yogurt with exactly 2 toppings be ordered at Tommie's Yogurt Shop?

b.   How many ways can a yogurt with up to n toppings be ordered at Tommie's Yogurt Shop?

DISCUSSION

The Solve an Equivalent Problem strategy is helpful when you can recall a similar problem previously solved or when you can find an equivalent problem that is easier to solve. For example, in trying to find the number of terms in the sequence 4, 11, 18, 25, ..., 487, you could look at the corresponding sequence 7, 14, 21, 28, ..., 490 and more easily conclude that there are 70 terms.

CLUES

The Solve an Equivalent Problem strategy may be appropriate when:

*   You can find an equivalent problem that is easier to solve.
*   A problem is related to another problem you have previously solved.
*   A problem can be represented in a more familiar setting.
*   A geometric problem can be represented algebraically or vice versa.
*   Physical problems can be easily represented with numbers or symbols.

PRACTICE PROBLEMS

Problem:	What is the 100th term in the sequence shown below?

13   20   27   34   41   . . .

Solution: Solve an Equivalent Problem

One way to solve this problem is to look at a similar sequence.

Given sequence:	13	20	27	34	. . .
Similar sequence:	14	21	28	35	. . .
Another sequence:	7	14	21	28	. . .

It is easy to show that the 100th term in the last sequence is 700. Why? Thus, the 100th term in the given sequence is 706.

11–A. In how many different ways could five players of the girls' basketball team be paired up to dance with five players on the boys' basketball team?

11–B. In how many ways can a committee of two be selected from a group of eight girls?

MIXED STRATEGY PRACTICE

PROBLEM-SOLVING STRATEGIES

1. Guess and Test
2. Use a Variable
3. Look for a Pattern
4. Make a List
5. Solve a Simpler Problem
6. Draw a Picture
7. Draw a Diagram
8. Use Direct Reasoning
9. Use Indirect Reasoning
10. Use Properties of Numbers
11. Solve an Equivalent Problem

11-1. I am thinking of 3 different counting numbers. The smallest number is 2 less than half the largest, the average of the 3 numbers is 13, and one of the numbers is a 2-digit prime. What are the numbers?

11-2. If it takes 5 cans of dog food to feed 4 dogs for one day, how many dogs can you feed for 4 days with 40 cans of dog food?

11-3. All but five of my pets are cats.
All but five of my pets are rabbits.
All but four of my pets are dogs.
I have only cats, rabbits, and dogs.
How many pets do I have? What are they?

11-4. Three chips are hidden under 3 cups labeled X, Y, and Z.

Randy and Linda both know that the hidden chips were selected from a set of 2 blue and 3 red chips. After being shown only the chips under cups Y and Z, Randy was asked "What color is the chip under cup X?" He replied, "I can't tell for sure." Knowing Randy's reply, Linda was then shown the chips under cups X and Z. When asked for the color of the chip under cup Y, she said, "I can't tell for sure." Explain why the chip under cup Z must be red.

12

Work Backward

Kay and Jim are playing a game in which they take turns removing either one or two chips from a pile of chips. The person who removes the last chip loses the game. Suppose it is Kay's turn and there are 17 chips left. Find a strategy that will make her a sure winner.

your turn

SOLUTION

Problem: Kay and Jim are playing a game in which they take turns removing either one or two chips from a pile of chips. The person who removes the last chip loses the game. Suppose it is Kay's turn and there are 17 chips left. Find a strategy that will make her a sure winner.

Solution: We start by looking at the end of the game. If it is Jim's turn when only one chip is left, he will have to remove the last chip and lose the game. Working back, suppose there are 4 chips left and it is Jim's turn. If he takes one chip, Kay should then take 2; if he takes 2 chips, Kay should take one. In either case, Jim must take the last chip making Kay the winner. Continuing to work backward, it can be shown that if there are 7, 10, 13, or 16 chips left when it is Jim's turn, Kay can be a sure winner.

a.   What is it about this problem that suggests the Work Backward strategy?
b.   In playing this game, would you want to be the first player if there are 28 chips at the start ? Why or why not?
c.   Can the first player always win? Explain.
d.   Suppose the rules are changed so that the player removing the last chip is the winner. Find a winning strategy.

DISCUSSION

Some problems are more easily solved by working backward from the end result to the initial condition. For example, consider this problem: How much money did Adam have to start with if he ended up with $6.25 after spending $3.00 more than half his savings to buy a shirt? By working backward from $6.25 it is easily seen that he spent $9.25. But this is half his savings. Thus, he started with $18.50.

CLUES

The Work Backward strategy may be appropriate when:

*   The final result is clear and the initial portion of a problem is obscure.
*   A problem proceeds from being complex initially to being simple at the end.
*   A direct approach involves a complicated equation.
*   A problem involves a sequence of reversible actions.

PRACTICE PROBLEMS

Problem: Helen paid 25 cents for a bag of jellybeans. After giving her brother half the beans, she ate 13. Her sister then ate one more than half the remaining beans, after which there were 3 left. How many jellybeans were in the bag before it was opened?

Solution: Work Backward

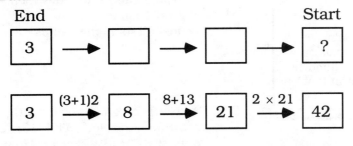

The figure above represents a solution to the problem. Try to explain each step as you work backward from the end result.

12-A. Two cans X and Y both contain some water. From X Tim pours as much water into Y as Y already contains. Then from Y he pours as much water into X as X presently has. Finally, he pours from X into Y as much water as Y presently has. Each can now contains 24 ounces of water. How many ounces of water were in each can at the start?

12-B. Karen spent all but $8.00 of her savings in three stores. In each store she spent $2.00 less than half of what she had when she went in. How much money did Karen have at the start?

MIXED STRATEGY PRACTICE

PROBLEM-SOLVING STRATEGIES

1. Guess and Test
2. Use a Variable
3. Look for a Pattern
4. Make a List
5. Solve a Simpler Problem
6. Draw a Picture
7. Draw a Diagram
8. Use Direct Reasoning
9. Use Indirect Reasoning
10. Use Properties of Numbers
11. Solve an Equivalent Problem
12. Work Backward

12–1. Four teams (A, B, C, D) in the all-star basketball league played each other at home and away. Use the clues below to find the won/lost record for each team.

A won all of its home games.
D never defeated C.
C won 3 games, one of which was at home.
B won 4 games.
D lost all its home games.

12–2. A group of girls is standing equally spaced around a circle. The 43rd girl is directly opposite the 89th girl. How many girls are there?

12–3. In a group of 60 middle school students, 26 are boys, 26 are in grade eight, and 15 are neither 7th nor 8th graders. Of the girls, 9 are in grade seven, and 12 are in grade eight. How many boys in the group are in the seventh grade?

12–4. Use the number line shown below to help you find the number between x and y that is twice as far from 3/8 as half of 5/6 is from 2/3.

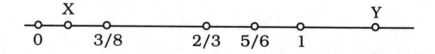

X   Y

0   3/8   2/3   5/6   1

13

Use Cases

A 23 member university committee consists of freshmen, sophomores, juniors, seniors, and graduate students. Each class is represented by a different number of students and each has at least one student on the committee. The freshmen and seniors total 9, the sophomores and seniors total 13, and the senior and graduate students total 8. Find the number of committee members from each class if one of the classes is represented by 5 students.

SOLUTION

Problem: A 23 member university committee consists of freshmen, sophomores, juniors, seniors, and graduate students. Each class is represented by a different number of students and each has at least one student on the committee. The freshmen and seniors total 9, the sophomores and seniors total 13, and the senior and graduate students total 8. Find the number of committee members from each class if one of the classes is represented by 5 students.

Solution: Since one of the classes is represented by 5 students, we can solve this problem by looking at several cases. Suppose there are 5 freshmen on the committee. This means that there will be 4 seniors and 4 graduate students. The case with 5 graduate students on the committee means that there would be 3 seniors, 6 freshmen, and 10 sophomores. Explain why neither of these cases leads to a solution. Continuing in this way, it can be shown that the committee consists of 3 freshmen, 7 sophomores, 5 juniors, 6 seniors, and 2 graduate students.

a. What is it about this problem that suggests the Use Cases strategy?
b. Show why there cannot be exactly 5 sophomores or exactly 5 seniors on the committee.
c. Show why there cannot be 5 juniors and 7 seniors on the committee.

DISCUSSION

Problems can often be solved by considering various cases. For example, in trying to find the numbers for which the inequality $(x + 2)(x - 1)>0$ is true, we need only consider the cases where $(x + 2)$ and $(x - 1)$ are both positive or both negative. If $(x + 2)>0$ and $(x - 1)>0$, then $x >1$. If $(x + 2)<0$ and $(x - 1)<0$, then $x<-2$. Therefore, $(x + 2)(x - 1)>0$ when $x >1$ or $x<-2$.

CLUES

The Use Cases strategy may be appropriate when:

*   A problem can be separated into several distinct cases.
*   A problem involves distinct collections of numbers like odds and evens, primes and composite, positives and negatives, etc.
*   Investigations in specific cases can be generalized.

PRACTICE PROBLEMS

Problem:	If x and y are integers, when will $x^2 + xy + (x - y)$ be odd?

Solution: Use Cases

	x	y	x^2	xy	$x - y$	$x^2 + xy + (x - y)$
Case 1	odd	odd	odd	odd	even	even
Case 2	odd	even	odd	even	odd	even
Case 3	even	odd	even	even	odd	odd
Case 4	even	even	even	even	even	even

Hence, $x^2 + xy + (x - y)$ is odd when x is even and y is odd.

13–A. A hexomino consists of 6 congruent squares joined at complete sides. For example,

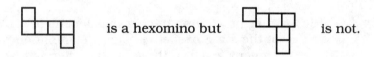

is a hexomino but   is not.

Find all the hexominoes that have exactly 4 squares in a line.

13–B. Cody has a collection of baseball cards. Is it possible for him to place the cards into 5 boxes so that exactly 3 of the boxes contain an odd number of cards and the total number of cards in two of the boxes is the same as the total number in the other 3 boxes? Explain.

MIXED STRATEGY PRACTICE

13–1. A sport shop is having a "30% off" sale on tennis balls and racquet balls. Tennis balls are sold in cans of 3 balls and racquet balls are sold in cans of 2 balls. One customer bought 49 balls. How many tennis balls did she buy if she left the store with 19 cans?

13–2. How many children are there in a family where each girl has as many brothers as sisters, but each boy has twice as many sisters as brothers?

13–3. After previewing the pairings for the first round of the state basketball single elimination tournament, each of three sportswriters chose the teams that they thought would win in the first round. Fridley was the only team not picked to win by any of the writers. The predictions were as follows:

Sportswriter #1: Duluth, Cambridge, Alexandria, St. Cloud
Sportswriter #2: Edina, Alexandria, Mankato, Cambridge
Sportswriter #3: St. Cloud, Mankato, Alexandria, Hopkins

Find the pairings for the first round of the tournament.

13–4. There are 2 piles with 4 chips in each pile. Two players take turns removing either one chip from one of the piles or one chip from each of the 2 piles. The winner is the player that removes the last chip. Find a winning strategy for this game.

14

Solve an Equation

A marching band needs to raise $13,500 for a trip to the Rose Bowl. The director told the band members that one-third of the amount that has been raised so far is equal to half of the amount that is still needed. How much more money needs to be raised for the trip?

SOLUTION

Problem: A marching band needs to raise $13,500 for a trip to the Rose Bowl. The director told the band members that one-third of the amount that has been raised so far is equal to half of the amount that is still needed. How much more money needs to be raised for the trip?

Solution: Let x = the amount of money that still needs to be raised. Thus, the amount raised so far is $13,500 − x$. Hence we have

$$\frac{1}{2}x = \frac{1}{3}(13{,}500 - x)$$
$$3x = 2(13{,}500 - x)$$
$$3x = 27{,}000 - 2x$$
$$5x = 27{,}000$$
$$x = 5{,}400$$

Therefore, $5,400 still needs to be raised.

a.   Why does $13,500 − x represent the amount of money that has been raised so far?
b.   What equation results if we start by letting y equal the amount of money raised so far?
c.   Explain why Guess and Test is not an appropriate strategy in solving this problem.

DISCUSSION

Many problems can best be solved by introducing a variable and then representing the given information with an equation. For example, consider the following problem:

What is Andrew's weight if he weighs 44 pounds plus half his weight?

If n is Andrew's weight, then the problem suggests the equation $n = 44 + \dfrac{n}{2}$.

Solving for n yields that Andrew weighs 88 pounds.

CLUES

The Solve an Equation strategy may be appropriate when:

*   A variable has been introduced.
*   The words "is", "is equal to", or "equals" appear in a problem.
*   The stated conditions can easily be represented with an equation.

PRACTICE PROBLEMS

Problem: Find three pairs of nonzero numbers x and y where one–half their sums equals twice their product.

Solution: Solve an Equation

Half the sum = twice the product $\frac{1}{2}(x + y) = 2xy$

Therefore, $y = \dfrac{x}{(4x - 1)}.$ Verify.

Let $x = 1$. Then $y = \frac{1}{3}$.   Check: $\frac{1}{2}\left(1 + \frac{1}{3}\right) = \frac{2}{3} = 2(1)\left(\frac{1}{3}\right)$

Let $x = 2$. Then $y = \frac{2}{7}$.   Check: $\frac{1}{2}\left(2 + \frac{2}{7}\right) = \frac{8}{7} = 2(2)\left(\frac{2}{7}\right)$

An infinite number of pairs (x, y) satisfy the conditions.

14–A.   Traveling at a certain speed, it took Mark 5 hours to drive from his home to Denver. If he had driven 2 miles per hour faster, he would have arrived in Denver 12 minutes earlier. How far is it from Mark's home to Denver?

14–B.   Katie: "Think of a number. Add 6. Multiply by 5. Subtract 28. Double it. Add 16. Multiply by 5. Subtract 50. Double it. Now tell me your result."

Jeff: "900."

Katie quickly found the original number selected by Jeff. Explain her method.

56

MIXED STRATEGY PRACTICE

PROBLEM-SOLVING STRATEGIES

1. Guess and Test
2. Use a Variable
3. Look for a Pattern
4. Make a List
5. Solve a Simpler Problem
6. Draw a Picture
7. Draw a Diagram
8. Use Direct Reasoning
9. Use Indirect Reasoning
10. Use Properties of Numbers
11. Solve an Equivalent Problem
12. Work Backward
13. Use Cases
14. Solve an Equation

14–1. Complete the following sequence so that, after the first two terms, each successive term is the average of all the preceding terms.

20 _____ _____ 28 _____ _____

14–2. There are 200 chips in a box. Some are red, some are white, and some are blue. Each chip is marked with either an odd number or an even number. There are 23 red–even chips, 14 blue–odd chips, 140 even chips, and 42 of the 72 white chips are white–even. How many chips in the box are red–odd? How many chips in the box are blue–even?

14–3. Jane saved one quarter in March of 1984. Each month after that she saved 2 more quarters than she had saved the month before. If Jane continued saving quarters in this way, how much money, in dollars, would she have had at the end of February, 1989?

14–4. The Kennedy Pep Club rented a bus to take all of its members to a baseball game. The cost per person was to be $18.00. However, those making the trip had to pay $24.00 each because 10 members cancelled out at the last minute. How many pep club members took the bus to the game?

15

Look for a Formula

A certain ball is dropped from an altitude of 1 meter and rebounds one–half of its previous altitude. What is the total distance the ball has traveled when it hits the floor the 40th time?

SOLUTION

Problem: A certain ball is dropped from an altitude of 1 meter and rebounds one–half of its previous altitude. What is the total distance the ball has traveled when it hits the floor the 40th time?

Solution: Consider the following representation:

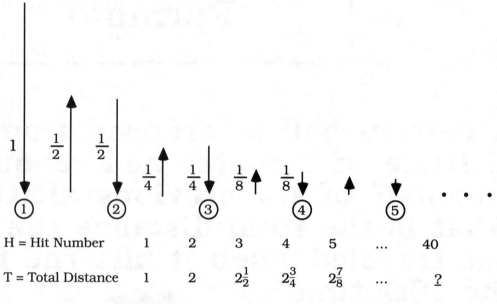

H = Hit Number	1	2	3	4	5	...	40
T = Total Distance	1	2	$2\frac{1}{2}$	$2\frac{3}{4}$	$2\frac{7}{8}$	...	?

The pattern suggests that $T = 2 + \dfrac{2^{38} - 1}{2^{38}}$ when H = 40.

a.   Write the general term that represents the total distance the ball has traveled when it hits the floor the *n*th time.

b.   Will the total distance traveled by the ball ever be 3 meters? Explain.

DISCUSSION

Problems can often be solved by directly applying a formula with which we are familiar. For example, in trying to determine how long it will take to drive 450 miles while averaging 60 mph, we can use the formula $d = rt$ (d = distance, r = rate, t = time) to show that it takes 7.5 hours. There are also many situations where we must look for a "new" formula. Problems of this type often involve a number pattern. For example, when asked to find the 60th term in the sequence 2, 5, 8, 11, 14, ... we can conclude that it is 179 since the formula for the *n*th term is $3n - 1$.

CLUES

The Look for a Formula strategy may be appropriate when:

*   A problem suggests a pattern that can be generalized.
*   Ideas such as percent, rate, distance, area, volume, or other measurable attributes are involved.
*   Applications in science, business, etc. are involved.
*   Solving problems involving topics like statistics, probability, etc.

PRACTICE PROBLEMS

Problem: What is the nth term in the sequence shown below when n is an even number?

$$\frac{1}{4} \qquad \frac{1}{2} \qquad \frac{1}{16} \qquad \frac{1}{8} \qquad \frac{1}{64} \qquad \frac{1}{32} \qquad \cdots$$

Solution: Look for a Formula

Note that the denominators are all powers of 2 and every numerator is 1.

Term number:	1	2	3	4	5	6	
Denominator:	$4 = 2^2$	$2 = 2^1$	$16 = 2^4$	$8 = 2^3$	$64 = 2^6$	$32 = 2^5$	$\cdots$

The pattern suggests that the nth term is $\left(\frac{1}{2}\right)^{n-1}$ when n is even. Why?

15–A.   Find the 99th term in each sequence shown below.

     a.   3   7   11   15   19 $\cdots$

     b.   8   16   32   64   128 $\cdots$

     c.   2   6   12   20   30 $\cdots$

15–B.   A bottle contains one gallon of water. At 6 A.M. half the water is removed. At 7 A.M. half of the remaining water is removed. If this process of removing half the remaining water each hour continues, how much water will remain in the bottle at 11:30 A.M. the next day?

MIXED STRATEGY PRACTICE

PROBLEM-SOLVING STRATEGIES

1. Guess and Test
2. Use a Variable
3. Look for a Pattern
4. Make a List
5. Solve a Simpler Problem
6. Draw a Picture
7. Draw a Diagram
8. Use Direct Reasoning
9. Use Indirect Reasoning
10. Use Properties of Numbers
11. Solve an Equivalent Problem
12. Work Backward
13. Use Cases
14. Solve an Equation
15. Look for a Formula

15–1. Find the sum of the 77 consecutive counting numbers whose first and last terms add up to 108.

15–2. Five percent of the students enrolled at a university were asked the question "Do you like math?" Of those surveyed, 1/3 were freshmen, 1/5 were sophomores, 1/6 were juniors, 1/4 were seniors, and 43 were graduate students. How many students are enrolled at the university?

15–3. Suppose a train traveling 90 miles per hour takes four seconds to enter a tunnel. From there it takes one minute before the train is completely outside the tunnel. Find the length of both the train and the tunnel.

15–4. A snail is at the bottom of a barrel and wants to climb out. It climbs half–way up the side of the barrel during the first hour, 1/3 of the remaining distance the second hour, 1/4 of the remaining distance the third, 1/5 of the remaining distance the fourth hour, and so on. If the snail continues in this way, how far from the top of the 96 centimeter high barrel will it be after 23 hours?

16

Do a Simulation

The Cardinal baseball team is batting in the bottom of the ninth inning. The bases are loaded, there are 2 out, the score is tied, and Casey is at bat. Coach Robinson calls time out and tells Casey not to swing at any of the pitches since he knows that the pitcher throws strikes only 40% of the time. Conduct a simulation that will help you form an opinion about Coach Robinson's decision.

SOLUTION

Problem: The Cardinal baseball team is batting in the bottom of the ninth inning. The bases are loaded, there are 2 out, the score is tied, and Casey is at bat. Coach Robinson calls time out and tells Casey not to swing at any of the pitches since he knows that the pitcher throws strikes only 40% of the time. Conduct a simulation that will help you form an opinion about Coach Robinson's decision.

Solution: A random number table is one device that can be used to simulate this problem. Let the one–digit numbers 0, 1, 2, and 3 represent a strike and let each of the other digits represent a ball. One trial consists of reading the digits until you get either 3 strikes or 4 balls. Three strikes means that the game will go into extra innings. Four balls means that the Cardinals will win the game. For example, consider the random digits shown below.

```
0 1 9 0 | 7 7 2 1 4 6 | 0 5 7 6 4 | 2 2 4 0 | 0 2 7 4 1
S S B S | B B S S B B | S B B B B | S S B S | S S B B S
              WIN                  WIN
```

a. Why is this assignment of digits representing strikes and balls appropriate?
b. Describe an experiment that will simulate the problem by using a spinner or by using colored chips.
c. Could a random number table have been used as a model for a pitcher that throws strikes 45% of the time? If so, describe a method. If not, why not?

DISCUSSION

Problems that are too difficult to be analyzed theoretically can sometimes be simulated by repeatedly performing an experiment yielding data which can be used to estimate an answer. Materials used in doing a simulation may consist of random number tables, dice, colored chips, slips of paper, coins, a calculator with a random number generator, or a computer. For example, an experiment that involves many tosses of 5 coins where the number of heads (girls) and the number of tails (boys) are recorded can be used to estimate the probability that a family of 5 children consists of more girls than boys.

CLUES

The Do a Simulation strategy may be appropriate when:

*   A problem involves a complicated probability experiment.
*   An actual experiment is too difficult or impossible to perform.
*   A problem has a repeatable process that can be done experimentally.
*   Finding the actual answer requires techniques not previously developed.

PRACTICE PROBLEMS

Problem:	Suppose a certain brand of frozen pizza has a prize in 30% of the packages. Conduct a simulation to estimate the average number of pizzas that must be purchased to win a prize.
Solution:	Do a Simulation
	The problem can be simulated by using a spinner. Make a spinner where a sector of the circle comprises 30% of the circle. Spin the spinner repeatedly and record the number of times it takes until you first fall into the 30% sector. Repeat the experiment 50 times. The average number of times it takes to fall into the 30% sector for the 50 trials estimates the expected number of pizzas you will have to buy in order to win a prize.

16–A. A game at a school carnival consists of 3 boxes (H, T, X) that contain either black or white chips as shown. A coin is tossed. If it is a head, a chip is randomly selected from box H and placed into box X. If it is a tail, a chip is randomly selected from box T and placed into box X. Then a chip is randomly selected from box X. To win a prize, the chip drawn from X must be white. Estimate the probability of winning a prize.

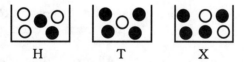

16–B. A mouse is placed in box X of the maze shown below. There is a mouse trap in box Y. What is the probability that the mouse will be trapped if it randomly moves either left, right, or up throughout the maze ?

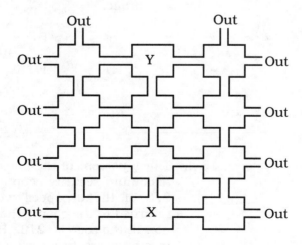

MIXED STRATEGY PRACTICE

PROBLEM-SOLVING STRATEGIES

1. Guess and Test
2. Use a Variable
3. Look for a Pattern
4. Make a List
5. Solve a Simpler Problem
6. Draw a Picture
7. Draw a Diagram
8. Use Direct Reasoning
9. Use Indirect Reasoning
10. Use Properties of Numbers
11. Solve an Equivalent Problem
12. Work Backward
13. Use Cases
14. Solve an Equation
15. Look for a Formula
16. Do a Simulation

16–1. How many 5–digit numbers are divisible by 50?

16–2. A married couple wants to have 3 or 4 children and they want exactly 2 girls. Is it more likely that they will have exactly two girls with three children or exactly two with four children?

16–3. Use the clues below to find the number represented by each letter.

* All are 1–digit even natural numbers.
* A + B + C = 14.
* The one perfect square is in the top row.
* A = F and D = E.
* The sum of C and F is 12.
* The sum of D, E, and F is not 20.
* The number before the only 4 is the only prime.

A	B	C
D	E	F

16–4. Thirty percent of the chickens escaped from a maximum security coop. After a long search, 2/3 of the escapees were recaptured and returned to the coop. The number of chickens now in the coop is 216. How many were there before the great escape?

17

Use a Model

All patterns shown below were formed by cutting along 4 edges of an open top cubical box. Label the square that was the bottom of the box and then determine how many side and/or bottom edges were cut to get the pattern. Two are done for you.

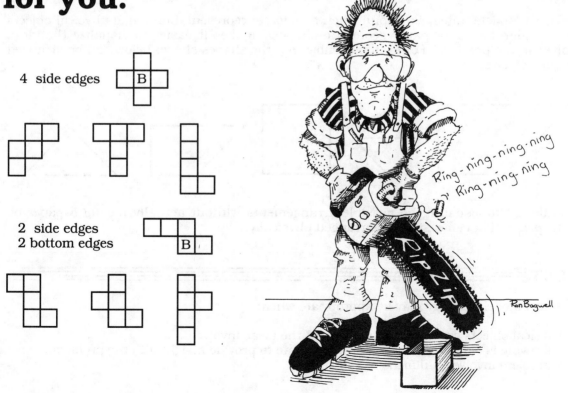

4 side edges

2 side edges
2 bottom edges

SOLUTION

Problem: All patterns shown below were formed by cutting along 4 edges of an open top cubical box.   Label the square that was the bottom of the box and then determine how many side and/or bottom edges were cut to get the pattern.   Two are done for you.

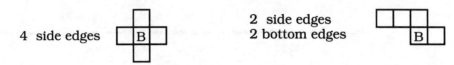

4 side edges

2 side edges
2 bottom edges

Solution: Cut out the patterns and fold them into cubes to verify that the bases are labeled correctly.

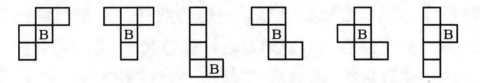

a.   Explain why the following patterns were not included in the figures shown above.

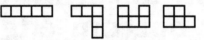

b.   What is a possible extension of this problem?

DISCUSSION

The Use a Model strategy is helpful when a concrete representation using physical objects (e.g.   wooden blocks or paper geometric shapes)   makes it easier to visualize the ideas involved in the problem.   For example, show how the shapes shown below can be arranged to form a square.

It is difficult to visualize the possible arrangements without actually having 5 paper or plastic pieces that can easily be rearranged physically.

CLUES

The Use a Model strategy may be appropriate when:

*   Physical objects can be used to represent the ideas involved.
*   A drawing is either too complex or inadequate to provide insight into the problem.
*   A problem involves 3–dimensional objects.

PRACTICE PROBLEMS

Problem: Show how a 12 × 12 × 12 inch cube can be cut into 36 smaller cubes if the lengths of the edges of the smaller cubes must all be whole numbers.

Solution: Use a Model

Cut two 3 inch layers off the top of the cube.
Each of these pieces can then be cut into 16
smaller 3 × 3 inch cubes.
The remaining piece is 6 × 12 × 12 inches.
This piece can be cut into 4 cubes that
are each 6 × 6 × 6 inches.

This gives us 36 smaller cubes. (16 + 16 + 4 = 36)

17–A.   How many different surface areas are possible when 8 one inch cubes are arranged so that each has one or more faces in common (touching) with at least one of the other cubes?

17–B.   The square in Figure I was cut into 4 pieces as shown and then the pieces were arranged to form Figure II.   Clearly, the square has area 16 × 16 or 256 square units.   Notice that Figure II appears to be a rectangle with area 10 × 26 or 260 square units.   Try to explain why these areas are different.

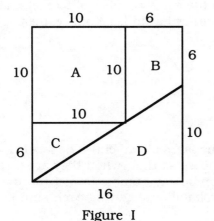

Figure I

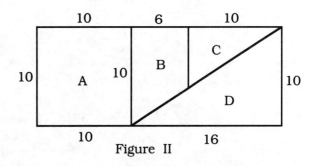

Figure II

MIXED STRATEGY PRACTICE

17–1. The surface of a cube is painted red. The cube is then cut into equal sized smaller cubes, 24 of which have only one red face. How many of the smaller cubes have two red faces? No red faces?

17–2. Sandy has a collection of nickels and dimes. The nickels can be put into piles so that the number of nickels is the same as the number of piles. Also, the dimes can be put into piles so that the number of dimes in each pile is the same as the number of piles. Which of the following could not be the total value of Sandy's coin collection?

a. $3.40   b. $5.35   c. $3.00   d. $6.05

17–3. Assume that there are more turkeys in Minnesota than there are feathers on any one turkey. Show that at least two of these turkeys must have the same number of feathers, given that each turkey has at least one feather.

17–4. How can the faces of two cubes be labeled with whole numbers so that, when they are tossed, the sum can be any number from 1 through 12 and the probability of getting each sum is the same?

18

Use Dimensional Analysis

In a horse race, Kentucky Prancer ran 6 furlongs in 1 minute and 6 seconds. Express Kentucky Prancer's rate in miles per hour and in feet per second. (Note: 1 mile = 8 furlongs.)

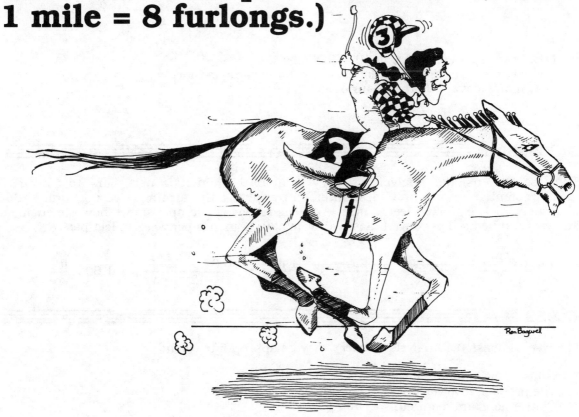

SOLUTION

Problem: In a horse race, Kentucky Prancer ran 6 furlongs in 1 minute and 6 seconds. Express Kentucky Prancer's rate in miles per hour and in feet per second. (Note: 1 mi = 8 fur.)

Solution: First, $6 \text{ seconds} = 6 \text{ sec} \times \dfrac{1 \text{ min}}{60 \text{ sec}} = 0.1 \text{ minutes}$, so

1 minute and 6 seconds = 1.1 minutes

$$\frac{6 \text{ fur}}{1.1 \text{ min}} = \frac{6 \text{ fur}}{1.1 \text{ min}} \times \frac{1 \text{ mi}}{8 \text{ fur}} \times \frac{60 \text{ min}}{1 \text{ hr}}$$

$$= \frac{6 \times 60}{1.1 \times 8} \frac{\text{mi}}{\text{hr}} \approx 40.91 \frac{\text{mi}}{\text{hr}}$$

Therefore, 6 furlongs/1.1 minutes is about 40.91 miles/hour.

$$\frac{40.91 \text{ mi}}{1 \text{ hr}} = \frac{40.91 \text{ mi}}{1 \text{ hr}} \times \frac{1 \text{ hr}}{60 \text{ min}} \times \frac{1 \text{ min}}{60 \text{ sec}} \times \frac{5280 \text{ ft}}{1 \text{ mi}}$$

$$= \frac{40.91 \times 5280}{60 \times 60} \frac{\text{ft}}{\text{sec}} \approx 60 \frac{\text{ft}}{\text{sec}}$$

Therefore, 6 furlongs/1.1 minutes is about 60.00 feet/second.

a.   How many miles are there in 1000 furlongs?
b.   Some horse races are 5.5 furlongs. How many yards is that?
c.   How many feet are there in 6 furlongs?

DISCUSSION

The Use Dimensional Analysis strategy is helpful when it is necessary to convert a measurement from one unit to another. In applying the strategy, we use unit ratios equivalent to 1, e.g. 5280 feet/1 mile = 1. The following example shows how dimensional analysis can be used to convert a growth rate of 0.37 inches per week to feet per year.

$$\frac{0.37 \text{ in}}{1 \text{ wk}} = \frac{0.37 \text{ in}}{1 \text{ wk}} \times \frac{52 \text{ wk}}{1 \text{ yr}} \times \frac{1 \text{ ft}}{12 \text{ in}} = \frac{0.37 \times 52}{12} \frac{\text{ft}}{\text{yr}} \approx 1.603 \frac{\text{ft}}{\text{yr}}$$

CLUES

The Use Dimensional Analysis strategy may be appropriate when:

*   Units of measure are involved.
*   The problem involves physical quantities.
*   Conversions are required.

PRACTICE PROBLEMS ≡≡≡≡≡≡≡≡≡≡≡≡≡≡≡

Problem: Under normal conditions, the atmospheric pressure at sea level is about 14.7 pounds per square inch. What is the pressure in grams per square centimeter?

Solution: Use Dimensional Analysis

$1 \text{ kg} \approx 2.2 \text{ pounds}$

$1 \text{ in} = 2.54 \text{ cm},\ \text{ so }\ 1 \text{ in}^2 = (2.54)^2 \text{ cm}^2 = 6.4516 \text{ cm}^2$

$$\frac{14.7 \text{ lb}}{1 \text{ in}^2} \approx \frac{14.7 \,\cancel{\text{lb}}}{\cancel{1 \text{ in}^2}} \times \frac{\cancel{1 \text{ in}^2}}{6.45 \text{ cm}^2} \times \frac{1 \,\cancel{\text{kg}}}{2.2 \,\cancel{\text{lb}}} \times \frac{1000 \text{ g}}{1 \,\cancel{\text{kg}}}$$

$$\approx \frac{14.7 \times 1000}{6.45 \times 2.2} \ \frac{\text{g}}{\text{cm}^2}$$

$$\approx 1035.94 \ \frac{\text{g}}{\text{cm}^2}$$

Therefore, 14.7 pounds per sq. in. is about 1036 grams per cm^2.

18–A.   Find the exact number of meters in one mile using the fact that 1 inch equals 2.54 centimeters.

18–B.   The fuel consumption of a certain car is 24 miles per gallon. How many kilometers per liter is this? (1 mile $\approx$ 1.61 kilometers and 1 liter $\approx$ 1.06 quarts.)

MIXED STRATEGY PRACTICE

18-1. A certain brand of laundry soap is sold as either a liquid or a powder. A survey by the company that makes the soap revealed the following information.

* $\frac{2}{7}$ of those interviewed do not use the liquid.

* $\frac{1}{3}$ do not use the powder.

* 183 use both the liquid and the powder.

* $\frac{1}{5}$ do not use this brand of soap.

How many people were interviewed?

18-2. Find an efficient way to decide which of the numbers below is a term in the sequence 7, 16, 25, 34, 43, ...

1,200,000,301   1,100,201,301

18-3. On a balance scale, 3 red cubes and 1 white cube balance 3 blue cubes. Also, 1 red cube and 3 blue cubes balance 3 white cubes. How many blue cubes will balance 5 white cubes?

18-4. Mary has two 20 ounce cups full of water. She also has an empty 8 ounce cup and an empty 14 ounce cup. Using only these four cups, she wants to end up with exactly 6 ounces of water in each of the smaller cups. Without spilling a drop, how can this be done in six steps?

19

Identify Subgoals

Six men and two boys want to cross a river using a small raft that will carry either two boys or one man. How many times must the raft cross the river in order to get everybody to the other side?

SOLUTION

Problem: Six men and two boys want to cross a river using a small raft that will carry either two boys or one man. How many times must the raft cross the river in order to get everybody to the other side?

Solution: A subgoal is to find the number of crossings needed to get one man across the river and return the raft to the starting point.

The two boys cross. One boy brings the raft back. One man crosses. The other boy brings the raft back to the starting point. Now the raft is where it started and one man is across the river (4 crossings).

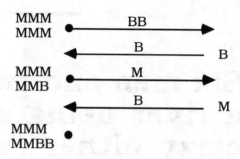

Therefore, it will take 24 (4 × 6) trips to move the six men across the river and have the raft back at the starting point. One additional crossing will be needed to get the two boys to the other side. Hence, it will take 25 crossings to get everyone to the other side of the river.

a.   How many crossings of the river would be needed if there were six men and four boys to start with?
b.   Would it be possible for six men and one boy to cross the river under the conditions stated in the problem? Why or why not?

DISCUSSION

Some problems can best be solved by first identifying one or more intermediate conditions or "subgoals" whose results may lead to a solution to the original problem. For example, in trying to find the sum of the numbers in the sequence 11, 16, 21, 36, 41, ... , 206, a subgoal is to find the number of terms in the sequence, namely 40. With this information, we can then proceed to show that the sum is 20 × 217, or 4,340. Explain why 20 × 217 yields the correct answer.

CLUES

The Identify Subgoals strategy may be appropriate when:

*   A problem can be broken down into a series of simpler problems.
*   The statement of the problem is very long and complex.
*   You can say "If I only knew ..., then I could solve the problem."
*   There is a simple, intermediate step that would be useful.
*   There is other information that you wished the problem contained.

PRACTICE PROBLEMS

Problem: Find the area of a regular hexagon that has a perimeter of 12 centimeters.

Solution: Identify Subgoals

A regular hexagon can be partitioned into six equilateral triangles. Therefore, a subgoal is to find the area of an equilateral triangle whose sides are 2 centimeters long.

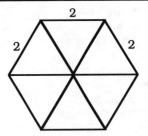

Area of the triangle $= \frac{1}{2} \times 2 \times \sqrt{3} = \sqrt{3}$ cm^2.

Hence, the area of the hexagon is $6\sqrt{3}$ cm^2.

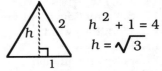

$$h^2 + 1 = 4$$
$$h = \sqrt{3}$$

19–A. The figure shown has a regular octagon adjacent to a regular pentagon. Find the measure of angle ABC.

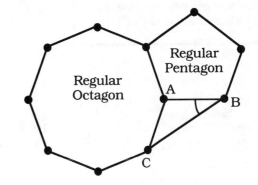

Regular Octagon

Regular Pentagon

19–B. How many ways are there to travel from X to Y if you must go either up or to the right along the lines?

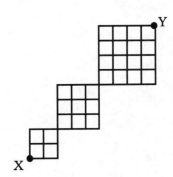

MIXED STRATEGY PRACTICE

PROBLEM-SOLVING STRATEGIES

1. Guess and Test
2. Use a Variable
3. Look for a Pattern
4. Make a List
5. Solve a Simpler Problem
6. Draw a Picture
7. Draw a Diagram
8. Use Direct Reasoning
9. Use Indirect Reasoning
10. Use Properties of Numbers
11. Solve an Equivalent Problem
12. Work Backward
13. Use Cases
14. Solve an Equation
15. Look for a Formula
16. Do a Simulation
17. Use a Model
18. Use Dimensional Analysis
19. Identify Subgoals

19–1. Tom and Scott ran a 400 meter race. When Scott was at the finish line, Tom was 20 meters behind. The next day they decided to run the same race, but Scott started 21 meters behind the starting line. If each one again runs at the previous rate, where will Scott be when Tom is 1 meter from the finish line? Who will win the race?

19–2. A baseball coach paid $81 for some jerseys and caps. If the jerseys cost $7 each and the caps cost $3 each, which of the following could be the ratio of jerseys to caps purchased?

   5:4   4:3   3:2   5:3   7:3

19–3. ABCD is a parallelogram. Show that if $\overline{AC}$ is a diagonal, then the area of region X must be equal to the area of region Y.

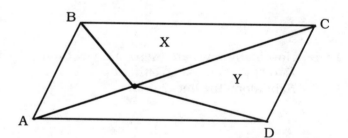

19–4. Find the number of feet in the perimeter of a rectangular playing field given that the area is 312 square yards, the longest side, in feet, is 3 less than a perfect square, and the length and width are whole numbers.

20

Use Coordinates

A scout troop is trying to find a secret message that is hidden at corner B of a field which is a parallelogram ABCD. Point A is 6 meters north and 30 meters east of the flagpole, point C is 54 meters north and 12 meters west of the pole, and point D is 18 meters north and 42 meters east of the pole. What is the location of the secret message?

SOLUTION

Problem: A scout troop is trying to find a secret message that is hidden at corner B of a field which is a parallelogram ABCD. Point A is 6 meters north and 30 meters east of the flagpole, point C is 54 meters north and 12 meters west of the pole, and point D is 18 meters north and 42 meters east of the pole. What is the location of the secret message?

Solution: Suppose the flagpole is at (0, 0).

Point A(30, 6)
Point C(–12, 54)
Point D(42, 18)
Point B(x, y)

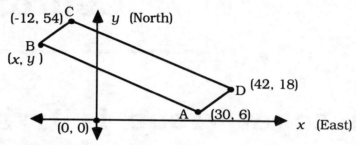

Since ABCD is a parallelogram, its opposite sides must be parallel. This means that the slope of $\overline{AB}$ equals the slope of $\overline{CD}$, and the slope of $\overline{AD}$ equals the slope of $\overline{BC}$. Using this information, it can be shown that the hidden message is 42 meters north and 24 meters west of the flagpole.

a.   What is the slope of $\overline{AD}$? $\overline{BC}$? $\overline{CD}$?
b.   One way to solve this problem is to find the values of x and y when $(y - 54)/(x + 12) = 1$ and $(y - 6)/(x - 30) = -2/3$. Show why this is the case and then find the values for x and y.
c.   Show how this problem can be solved without using equations.

DISCUSSION

A two–dimensional coordinate system with the origin, (0,0), conveniently located is often helpful in solving geometric problems. For example, in trying to show that the diagonals of a rhombus are perpendicular bisectors of each other, we can start by representing its four vertices as shown. Then, using slope and midpoint formulas, we can solve the problem.

Note: $c^2 = a^2 - b^2$

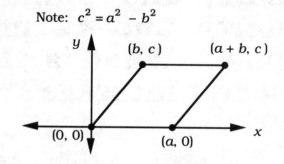

CLUES

The Use Coordinates strategy may be appropriate when:

*   A problem can be represented using two variables.
*   A geometry problem cannot easily be solved by using traditional Euclidean methods.
*   Finding representations of lines or conic sections.
*   A problem involves slope, parallel lines, perpendicular lines, etc.
*   The location of a geometric shape with respect to other shapes is important.
*   A problem involves maps.

PRACTICE PROBLEMS

Problem: Given a pentagon ABCDE.
Also, ABCD is a rectangle.

Show that $AE^2 + CE^2 = BE^2 + DE^2$

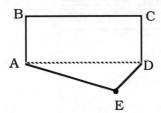

Solution: Use Coordinates

Using coordinates, we can position the pentagon as shown.

$AE^2 = x^2 + y^2$
$CE^2 = (a - x)^2 + (b - y)^2$

$BE^2 = x^2 + (b - y)^2$
$DE^2 = (a - x)^2 + y^2$

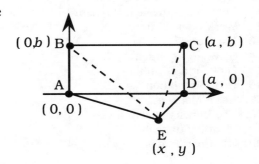

Therefore, $AE^2 + CE^2 = BE^2 + DE^2$.

20–A.   Find the area of the quadrilateral ABCD which has its vertices at points A (–2, 1), B (2, 3), C (1, 1), and D (3, –1).

20–B.   Suppose triangle ABC has vertices (r, s), $(r + 1, s + 7)$, and $(r - 3, s + 4)$. Show that it is an isosceles right triangle and find its area.

MIXED STRATEGY PRACTICE

PROBLEM-SOLVING
STRATEGIES

1. Guess and Test
2. Use a Variable
3. Look for a Pattern
4. Make a List
5. Solve a Simpler Problem
6. Draw a Picture
7. Draw a Diagram
8. Use Direct Reasoning
9. Use Indirect Reasoning
10. Use Properties of Numbers
11. Solve an Equivalent Problem
12. Work Backward
13. Use Cases
14. Solve an Equation
15. Look for a Formula
16. Do a Simulation
17. Use a Model
18. Use Dimensional Analysis
19. Identify Subgoals
20. Use Coordinates

20–1. While riding a bicycle from her home to Janesville, Jane traveled 1/2 the distance at 18 mph, 1/3 the distance at 8 mph, and 1/6 the distance at 3 mph. What was Jane's average speed for the trip?

20–2. A taxi, a limousine, and a bus travel from the airport to the Regency Hotel 24 hours a day. A taxi leaves every 15 minutes, a limousine leaves every 28 minutes, and a bus leaves every 40 minutes. If each type of vehicle leaves the airport at 9 A.M. on Monday, at what time will they leave the airport together on the following Friday?

20–3. There are two sets of railroad tracks between Kenyon and Riverdale. Every hour, on the hour, a train leaves each city for the other city. The trains always travel at the same rate and the trip from one city to the other takes 5 hours. How many trains will be met by a train traveling from Kenyon to Riverdale?

20–4. Suppose you have two pieces of rope that have different lengths. Show how to cut one of the pieces so that one of the resulting 3 pieces has a length which is the same as the average length of the other two pieces.

21

Use Symmetry

How many different ways can the above squares be arranged as a 3 by 3 square which has exactly one line of symmetry?

SOLUTION

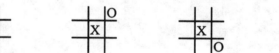

Problem: How many different ways can the above squares be arranged as a 3 by 3 square which has exactly one line of symmetry?

Solution: The ten 3 by 3 arrays shown below represent all the different ways where there is exactly one line of symmetry.

a. Draw the line of symmetry in each 3 by 3 array above.
b. Is it possible to arrange the nine squares so that there are exactly 2 lines of symmetry? Exactly 4 lines of symmetry?

DISCUSSION

Some problems can more easily be analyzed by using symmetry. Geometrical symmetry may involve slides, turns, or flips. For example, the results of the first two plays on the tic–tac–toe boards shown below are equivalent by rotational symmetry.

Numerical symmetries can also be helpful in solving certain types of problems. For example, if a whole number has an even number of digits and is symmetric, such as 123,321, then it is divisible by 11. Explain why.

CLUES

The Use Symmetry strategy may be appropriate when:

* Geometry problems involve transformations.
* Interchanging values does not change the representation of the problem.
* Symmetry limits the number of cases that need to be considered.
* Pictures or algebraic procedures appear to be symmetric.

PRACTICE PROBLEMS

Problem:	Suppose triangle ABC has its vertices at A (1, –1), B (4, –2), and C (–1, –4). Find the vertices of its mirror image when it is reflected about the line which has a slope of 1 and passes through the point (3, 4).

Solution: Use Symmetry

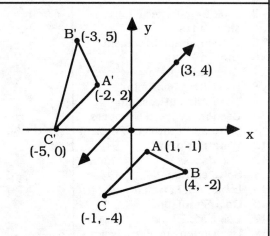

The figure at right shows the mirror image, triangle A'B'C', of triangle ABC reflected about the line. Explain how the coordinates of A', B', and C' can be determined from the given information.

21–A.   Two players take turns placing the same color marker on one of the dots shown on the playing board below. The winner is the first player that completes a string of 3 consecutive dots covered by a marker. Find a strategy so that the first player will always win.

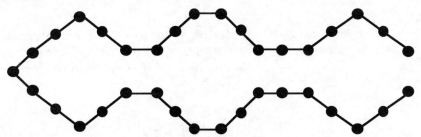

21–B.   Suppose a ball is placed at point X on the pool table represented below. A player wants to shoot the ball so that it goes into the corner pocket P after rebounding off cushion *r* and then off cushion *s*. Locate the points where the ball must hit each cushion.

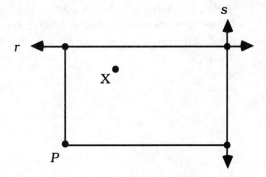

MIXED STRATEGY PRACTICE

21-1. Find the measure of each angle of a regular polygon that has 20 diagonals.

21-2. To estimate the number of fish in Lake George, 800 fish were caught, tagged, and then returned to the lake. Later that week, 150 fish were caught, 6 of which were tagged. Use this information to estimate the fish population of the lake.

21-3. Ralph paid $1.87 for some candy bars at a "20% to 40% off" sale. How many candy bars did he buy if they regularly sell for 25 cents each?

21-4. A horse is tied to the corner of a 30 foot by 50 foot barn with a 60 foot rope. If the horse can graze everywhere outside of the barn that the rope allows it to reach, what is the grazing area?

ADDITIONAL PRACTICE PROBLEMS ≡≡≡≡≡≡≡

1. Eight 4 inch by 6 inch pictures are to be mounted on a 21 inch by 31 inch rectangular sheet. Show how this can be done if the distance between the pictures must be the same as their distance from the edges of the sheet.

2. A can of cola and a can of root beer are each exactly half full. Two ounces of cola are poured into the can of root beer. Then two ounces of the mixture in the root beer can are poured back into the cola can. Is there now more cola in the root beer can or more root beer in the cola can? Explain.

3. The average of five natural numbers is 12. The average of 15 other natural numbers is 8. What is the average of all 20 numbers? Could one of the 20 numbers be 107? Explain.

4. The set {4, 6, 8, 10, 12, ..., 368} contains 183 elements. Verify.
    The set {7, 10, 13, 16, 19,..., 673} contains 223 elements. Verify.
    How many numbers are there in each of the sets below?
    a. {5, 6, 7, . . . , 803}   b. {-40, -37, -34, . . ., 221}   c. {17, 21, 25, . . . , 809}

5.   1=1   4=1+3   9=1+3+5   16=1+3+5+7   25=1+3+5+7+9   . . .
     Use the pattern suggested above to help you find the missing numbers.
     a. _____ = 1 + 3 + 5 + 7 + ... + 79 .
     b. 8,100 = 1 + 3 + 5 + 7 + ... + _____ .
     c. 3,136 is the sum of the first _____ odd whole numbers.
     d. 7 + 9 + 11 + 13 + ... + 97 + 99 = _____ .

6.   Each of three boxes X, Y, and Z contains at least one dozen eggs. The total number of
     eggs is 140 and there are half as many eggs in box Y as in box X. Also, box Z contains
     an odd number of eggs. What is the smallest number of eggs that could be in box Z?

7.   I am a proper fraction between 1/3 and 2/3. The sum of my numerator and
     denominator is a perfect square, and my denominator is a prime number which is 4 less
     than 3 times my numerator. Who am I?

8.   Let x, y, and z represent counting numbers. If x must be at least 900 and $x + (y + z) =$
     999, how many different ordered pairs of numbers (y, z) will satisfy the given
     conditions?

9. Jesse wants to run two laps around a 400 meter track at an average speed of 5 meters per second. How many meters per second must he average while running the second lap if he runs the first lap in:
   a. 60 seconds?
   b. 2 minutes and 40 seconds?

10. Use the given clues to find the number represented by each letter.

   A   B   C
   D   E   F

   - Each is a different 1-digit whole number.
   - All corner numbers are even natural numbers.
   - $B \times E = 15$
   - Half the sum of C and F is 3.
   - C is 2 less than D.
   - E is greater than C.

11. Glen runs 10 meters in the same time that Leo runs 8 meters. One day they ran around a 400 meter circular track. They started at the same place at the same time and they ran in opposite directions. What is Glen's location on the track when Leo passes the starting line the third time?

12. Troy, Dan, Carlos, and Willie are married to Melissa, Laura, Shelly, and Juanita. Use the clues to determine who is married to whom.
   - Shelly is Dan's sister.
   - Melissa is married to Carlos.
   - Juanita's husband is an only child.
   - Willie is not married to Shelly.

13. The EE-ZZ Cleaning Company offers the following salary options for its salespeople.
    Option A: $500 a month plus $30 for each vacuum cleaner sold
    Option B: $300 a month plus $50 for each vacuum cleaner sold
Under what conditions is it better to select Option B?

14. Carlotta uses 12 3/8 feet of ribbon to make 4 identical large bows and one small bow. Each large bow has twice as much ribbon as the small bow. How much ribbon was used to make the small bow? Each large bow?

15. Find the difference between the largest 5-digit perfect cube and the smallest 4-digit perfect square.

16. What is the sum of all multiples of 3 between 200 and 800?

17. Find the sum of the digits in the answer for each problem below.
    a. $55,555,555 \times 999,999,999$ b. $666,666,666,666,667^2$

18. Ken can beat Jim by 100 meters in a 1,000 meter race and Jim can beat Bob by 10 meters in a 100 meter race. If both run at the given rate, by how many meters will Ken beat Bob in a 1,000 meter race?

19. A farmer fenced a rectangular field of perimeter 340 meters. He then divided the field into two equal areas by constructing a fence diagonally across the field. All of the fence posts are 10 meters apart and the width of the field is 50 meters. How many fence posts did he use?

20. A pile of nickels, dimes, and quarters contains between 200 and 250 coins. One-ninth of the coins are quarters and 75% of the coins are dimes or quarters. What is the total value of all the coins?

21. Use the given clues to find the number represented by each letter.

$$
\begin{array}{ccc}
A & B & C \\
D & E & F
\end{array}
$$

- All are different counting numbers less than 100.
- Each corner number is a square less than 35.
- B + E equals the first prime number after 19
- A + D = F = A + B + C
- E = 2D

22. A 16" by 30" rectangular sheet is made into an open top box by first cutting identical squares from each corner and then folding up the sides. What is the largest possible volume of the box if the edge of each cut-out square, in inches, is a whole number?

23. Find the average of the first:
   a. 999 counting numbers
   b. 999 even natural numbers
   c. 999 odd whole numbers
   d. 999 numbers in the set {4,8,12,16,...}

24. Brenda leaves for work at 6:30 a.m. every weekday. If she averages 8 miles per hour from home to work, she will arrive 1/2 hour late. At a rate of 24 miles per hour, she will be one hour early. How far is it from Brenda's home to her place of work?

25. The distance between each of the posts in a fence along the property line is 2.5 meters. It is 195 meters from the fourth post to the last one. How many posts are in the fence?

26. A box contains cards which have a 3-digit number written on one side. Each number appears exactly one time and all 3-digit numbers are included. If you randomly select one of these cards from the box, what is the probability that the number on the card is a perfect square?

27. Find two numbers between 3/4 and 3 1/4 so that when the resulting four numbers are arranged in order, from smallest to largest, the difference between any two consecutive numbers is the same.

28. Tyrone sold 100 vehicles (cars, vans, and trucks) last year. He sold 58 used vehicles, 60 cars, 13 used vans, and two-thirds of the 21 trucks sold were used. How many of the new vehicles sold by Tyrone last year were either cars or vans?

29. Ted has a collection of stamps. He gave his sister one more than half of the stamps. Then he gave his brother one more than half of the remaining stamps. How many stamps did Ted have in his original collection if he ended up with four stamps?

30. Find all two-digit natural numbers where the ones digit is a multiple of four, the sum of the digits is prime, and the tens digit has three as a factor.

31. How many odd whole numbers less than 1,000 do not have the digit 3 in the ones place?

32. Three views of a single cube are shown.

What symbol is opposite the following?

(a)   (b)   (c)

33. A rectangular flower garden of dimensions 3 meters by 4 meters is to be bordered by a walk made of square tiles, each of which has a perimeter of 80 centimeters. How many of these square tiles will be needed to complete the job?

34. Andrew's and Beth's ages add up to 25. Beth's and Randy's ages add up to 29. Kathy's age is exactly halfway between the ages of Andrew and Randy. Also, Kathy's age is two less than half of 32. What is the sum of their ages?

35. Three men named Bob, Ken and John are in a boat. Bob always tells the truth, Ken tells the truth sometimes, and John never tells the truth. The man in the middle said, "I'm Ken," the man at the front of the boat said, "Bob is in the middle," and the man at the back said, "John is at the front end." Which one is in the middle of the boat?

36. a. There are 36 diplomats seated around a large round table. Each shakes hands with the person to the right and left. How many handshakes were there?
   b. Every person at a meeting shook hands with everyone else exactly one time. How many people were at the meeting if there were a total of 78 handshakes?

37. Find the 999th digit after the decimal point.

    a. $0.\overline{2456}$ b. $0.\overline{142857}$ c. $0.27\overline{681}$ d. $0.03\overline{179286}$

38. There are between 50 and 100 books on a shelf. Twenty-five percent of the books are textbooks and one-ninth are workbooks. How many books are on the shelf?

39. Two boxes A and B each contain some nickels and some dimes. The ratios of dimes to nickels in A and B are 1 to 3 and 5 to 4, respectively. The total value of the dimes in both boxes is $2.90. Suppose all coins that are in box A are put into box B. What is the ratio of dimes to nickels that are now in box B?

40. Pencils and pens are on sale for 96 cents a dozen and 3 for 51 cents, respectively. Karen bought some of each. How many pencils did she buy if her change for a $5 bill was $3.60?

41. A.   1
     B.   3 5
     C.   7 9 11
     D.   13 15 17 19
     .
     .
     .
     Y.
     Z.

1. Find the sum of the numbers in set J.
2. What is the first number in set Z?
3. What is the average of the numbers in set T?
4. Which set has numbers whose sum is 8000?

42. On a number line, find all the numbers that are four times as far from 3/4 as half of 5/6 is from 7/16.

43. A certain triangle has sides whose lengths are whole numbers. Find the length of each side if its perimeter is 8 centimeters.

44. Equally spaced points are marked on a circle. How many different line segments can be drawn between them if the number of points is:
     a. 3?   b. 4?   c. 6?   d. 21?

45. A game at the state fair consists of two boxes labelled X and Y, 9 white balls, and 5 black balls. A player is allowed to place the balls into the boxes in any way. A coin is then tossed. If it lands heads up, a ball is selected from box X. Otherwise, the ball must be selected from box Y. To win a prize, the ball selected must be white. How should the balls be placed into the boxes so that the player has the best possible chance of winning a prize?

46. Starting at one corner, the boundary of a garden runs 20 meters east, 8 meters north, 26 meters west, and then straight back to the first corner. Find the area and the perimeter of the garden.

47. Juanita has 16 coins consisting of nickels, dimes, and quarters. Fourteen of her coins are not nickels and all but seven of her coins are quarters. How much money does she have?

48. Find the number of degrees between the hands of a clock when (i) it shows 3:40 and (ii) it shows 2:20.

49. I am a 2-digit number between 21 and 61. My ones digit is a multiple of my tens digit and I am five less than a perfect square. Who am I?

50. A 6 cm by 12 cm by 22 cm rectangular block of wood is painted red and then cut into small cubes, each of which has a surface area of 6 square centimeters. How many of the cubes have red paint on:
    a. Exactly 1 face?   b. Exactly 2 faces?   c. None of the faces?

51. A rectangular room has an area of 946 square feet. Its length is one foot less than twice its width. What are the dimensions of the room?

52. Use the clues below to help you find my telephone number.

$$\overline{}_{1} \quad \overline{}_{2} \quad \overline{}_{3} \quad - \quad \overline{}_{4} \quad \overline{}_{5} \quad \overline{}_{6} \quad \overline{}_{7}$$

   - The seven digits are all prime numbers.
   - The 1st, 4th, and 5th digits are even.
   - The 2nd and 3rd digits are factors of 35.
   - The 6th digit is 4 less than the 7th digit.
   - The sum of the digits is neither 28 nor 30.

53. Ten red, 9 blue, 8 white, and 7 green balls are in a box. Without looking, Heidi was asked to take some balls out of the box. What is the least number of balls she must take out to be sure of ending up with: 2 of the same color? 4 of the same color? 7 of the same color?

54. In a class of 48 students, 17 are neither men nor left-handed. Twenty-five of the students are men, and 37 of the students are not left-handed. How many women in the class are left-handed?

55. How many different rectangles are in the figure shown below?

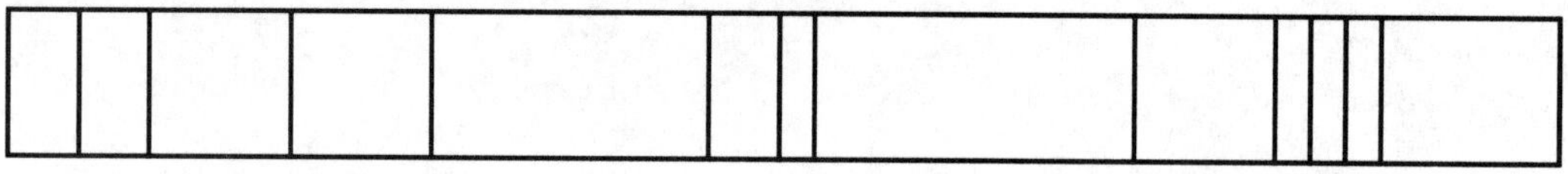

56. Gina's father said that she would get $130 and a new bicycle if she mows the lawn 30 times. After mowing the lawn 20 times, she got a new bike and $50. If this represents the total amount Gina has earned up to that time, what is the value of the bike?

57. A long table is formed by placing some square tables end-to-end. Two people can be seated along each side of the square tables. Using this arrangement, how many of the tables will be needed to seat exactly 128 people?

58. Jodi has a collection of nickels, dimes, and quarters worth $2.00. If the nickels were dimes and the dimes were nickels, the value of the coins would be $1.70. How many nickels does Jodi have?

59. A survey of 100 men showed the following: 80 own their homes, 85 are married, 75 own a car, 70 own a VCR. What is the least possible number of the men surveyed that could be married homeowners who own both a car and a VCR?

60. A circle is inscribed inside a square and then a circle is circumscribed outside the square. What is the ratio of the area of the inscribed circle to the area of the circumscribed circle?

61. Reggie normally makes 80% of his free throws during a basketball game. He is at the free throw line with a one-and-one situation with no time left during the final game in a tournament. His team is behind by one point. What is the probability that the game will go into overtime?

62. a. How many games must be played to determine a champion in the 64 team NCAA single elimination basketball tournament?
    b. How many games are played in the Pac Ten Conference, if each team plays all the other teams at home and away?
    c. What is the least possible number of games that must be played to determine a champion in an 8-team double elimination tournament?

63. A copy machine produces copies at a rate of 75 per minute. Another machine folds 5 copies every 12 seconds. How many folding machines will be needed to keep up with three copy machines?

64. Find the number of digits in the answer for each problem below:

    a. $2^{43} \times 5^{43}$ b. $2^{78} \times 5^{75}$ c. $2^{75} \times 5^{78}$ d. $41 \times 2^{39} \times 5^{42}$

65. In a group of cows, turkeys, and ducks, the number of legs is 44 more than the number of heads. What is the largest number of cows that could be in this group of animals?

66. In a gumball machine, one ball costs 5¢. There are six different colors of gumballs and there are nine balls of each color in the machine. What is the least amount of money that you would have to put into the machine to be sure of ending up with four gumballs of the same color?

67. I am a whole number between 40,000 and 50,000. When I am divided by 2, the result is a perfect square. When I am divided by 3, the answer is a perfect cube. Who am I?

68. Find the 3-digit number which satisfies all conditions stated below:
    * The sum of the digits is 13.
    * The product of the digits is greater than 60.
    * The sum of the tens and hundreds digits is less than the ones digit.
    * The number is between 300 and 400.

69. A half-mile long train was traveling 45 mph while entering a one mile long tunnel at 1:15 p.m. How long, in seconds, will it take until the end of the last car in the train first reaches daylight?

70. Write a one-digit number in each blank space of row Y so that whenever a digit appears in row Y, the digit above it in row X appears that many times in row Y.

    Row X   0   1   2   3   4   5   6

    Row Y   ___   ___   ___   ___   ___   ___   ___

71. In how many different ways can 9 dimes be given to 4 people, if each person receives at least 1 dime? (Consider only amounts, not particular dimes.)

72. Find the measure of each angle of a regular polygon that has
    a. 2 diagonals   b. 5 diagonals   c. 9 diagonals   d. 35 diagonals

73. The gauge on a water tank shows 5/8 full. After 21 more gallons were drained, the gauge showed 1/3 full. How many gallons of water were in the tank when it was 1/2 full?

74. The difference between the squares of two consecutive odd counting numbers is 200. What are the numbers?

75. Jenny set her watch at 6 p.m. The next day, at 8 a.m., she noticed that it had gained 3 minutes. At this rate, how many minutes will her watch gain in two weeks?

76. Three candles of equal length were all lit at 10 p.m. Candle X takes 12 hours to burn out, candle Y takes 8 hours to burn out, and candle Z takes 6 hours to burn out.
    a. At what time will candle Y burn out?
    b. At what time will candle X be twice as long as candle Z?
    c. At what time will candle Y be half the length of candle X?
    d. At what time will candle Z be 80% as long as candle X?

77. The figures below show how two chords can divide a circle into either 3 or 4 regions.

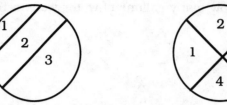

   a. Show how 3 chords of a circle can separate it into:
      4 regions   5 regions   6 regions   7 regions

   b. What is the largest possible number of regions formed when 8 chords are drawn across a circle?

78. Barb is 2 years younger than Ken, but she is older than Sam and Linda. Linda is 7 years younger than Barb. Sam's age is half of Barb's age, and Tim is 17 years old. The sum of the ages of the youngest two in the group is 8. Write the names of the five people, in order, from oldest to youngest. Also, find each person's age.

   _____   _____   _____   _____   _____
   Oldest   Youngest

79. A box containing two dozen paper clips weighs 77 grams. After 9 paper clips are removed, the weight is 59 grams. What is the total weight when the box contains only one paper clip?

80. How many different ways are there to get to the top of a five step stairway if you take either one, two, or three steps at a time?

81. During the months of November and December the Razzle Dazzle Store has income that averages five times as much as each of the other months during the year. Based on this average, what percent of the yearly income is made from October through December?

82. How can 12 trees be planted so that there are 6 rows of trees with 4 trees in each row?

83. Let A = {1, 2, 3, 4, . . . ,n }. Suppose the numbers in set A are to be separated into three disjoint sets B, C, and D so that the sum of the numbers in each of these sets is the same. Which of the following could *not* be a value for n?

    59   90   211   563   667

84. Della and Tess play a game in which they alternate selecting one of the following numbers: {1, 2, 3, 4}. After a number is selected, it is added to the sum of all the numbers previously selected. To win the game, a player must get exactly 41. If Della goes first, show how she can be a sure winner.

ANSWERS TO ODD NUMBERED PROBLEMS

Guess and Test

1-A. 42 meters by 68 meters

1-1.

15	6	9	4
10	3	16	5
8	13	2	11
1	12	7	14

1-3. 5 pencils and 10 erasers

Use a Variable

2-A. Ken: x Tom: $x+9$ Randy: $x+4$ Jill: $x+1$
$x + (x+9) + (x+4) + (x+1) = 4x + 14$
$4x + 14$ is even. Hence, $4x + 14$ cannot equal 45.

2-1. 1 Denominator: n Numerator: $(n+1)^2 - n(n+2) + (n-1) = n$ $n/n = 1$

2-3. x y z $(x+y+z)$ $(x+2y+2z)$ $(2x+3y+4z)$ $(4x+6y+7z)$ $(7x+11y+13z)$
Sum $= 16x + 24y + 28z = 4(4x + 6y + 7z)$

Look for a Pattern

3-A. Pattern of *s: $2^2 + 1$ $3^2 + (1+2)$ $4^2 + (1+2+3)$ $5^2 + (1+2+3+4)$
T is the 20th set. Thus, there are 651 *s in T.

3-1. a. 3 b. 7 c. 4 d. 9

3-3. a. $900 = 30^2$ b. 83 c. $3600 = 60^2$

Make a List

4-A.
66: 22 22 22	19 19 28	19 22 25
75: 25 25 25	28 28 19	22 25 28

4-1. a. 1, 2, 3, 5, 8, 13, 21   b. 6, –5, 1, –4, –3, –7, –10
c. 2,-1,1,0,1,1,2   d. 5, 6, 11, 17, 28, 45, 73

4-3. 429 (500 odd numbers less than 1,000. 142/2 = 71 are divisible by 7. 500-71 = 429)

Solve a Simpler Problem

5–A. 84 rectangles

5–1. 130 cm^2 (6.5 × 20 = 130)   Small rectangle: 2.5 × 4cm

5–3. The average of the missing numbers is 108. {10, 12, 14, ..., 206}
10: Average = 10;   10, 12: Average = 11;   10, 12, 14: Average = 12.
Hence, the 99 hidden numbers have an average of 108 (99 + 9).

Draw a Picture

6–A. The ball will be 6 feet above the ground.

6–1. 13 correct   4 incorrect   3 with no answer

6–3. Box Z: 9 marbles   (Box X: 18 marbles   Box Y: 9 marbles)

Draw a Diagram

7–A. 12 (Odd. Different digits. Greater than 700. Digits: 1, 2, 3, 5, 6, 7)
713   715   721   723   725   731   735   751   753   761   763   765

7–1. The 2 boys cross. One comes back. One man crosses. The other boy comes back.
The 2 boys cross again. One boy comes back. The 2nd man crosses. One boy
comes back. The 2 boys cross. All are now on the other side of the river.

7–3. 55 lines will be needed. (2 → 1   3 → 3   4 → 6   ...   11 → 55)

Use Direct Reasoning

8–A. A B C → 8 6 4   D E F → 2 7 0

8–1. Game 1: A, B → 3, 0   4, 1   5, 2   6, 3   7, 4   8, 5   9, 6   10, 7   11, 8
Game 2: A, B → 8, 9   7, 8   6, 7   5, 6   4, 5   3, 4   2, 3   1, 2   0, 1

8–3. He smoked 21 cigarettes the day before he started to cut back.
x ($x - 2$ $x - 4$ $x - 6$ $x - 8$ $x - 10$ $x - 12$ $x - 14$) $7x - 56 = 91$ $x = 21$

Use Indirect Reasoning

9-A. Suppose C is even. We know that the sum of the 5 consecutive counting numbers is odd. Thus, 3 of the 5 numbers must be odd. This means that when A+C+E is odd, B+C+D must be even. Hence, A+C+E cannot equal B+C+D when C is even. Thus, C is odd.

9-1. The farmer used 297 posts.

9-3. Lincoln:76   Kennedy:84   Jefferson:38   Madison:19

Use Properties of Numbers

10-A. The number is 823. ($8 \times 9 \times 11 = 792$.   Start with791. Then try 799. Then try 807. Continue until the pattern reaches 823.)

10-1. Jim has 27 rare coins in his collection. There were 6 cups.

10-3. There were 30 envelopes and 46 sheets in each box.

Solve an Equivalent Problem

11-A. 120 ways ($5 \times 4 \times 3 \times 2 \times 1$)

11-1. The numbers are 8, 11, and 20.

11-3. 7 pets   2 rabbits   2 cats   3 dogs

Work Backward

12-A. Pail X: 33 ounces   Pail Y: 15 ounces

12-1. Won/lost → A: 5/1   B: 4/2   C: 3/3   D: 0/6

12-3. Ten boys are 7th graders.

Use Cases

13-A.

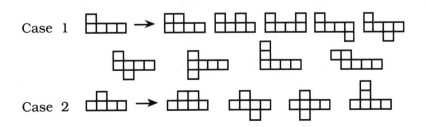

13-1. She bought 33 tennis balls (11 cans) and 16 racquet balls (8 cans).

13-3. Fridley/Alexendria, St. Cloud/Edina, Mankato/Duluth, Cambridge/Hopkins

Solve an Equation

14–A. 240 miles [$d = rt$ $5r = (24/5)(r + 2)$ $r = 48$ mph $d = 5 \times 48 = 240$ miles]

14–1. 20   36   28   28   28   28

14–3. Jane saved $900 during that time.

Look for a Formula

15–A. a. 395, $4n-1$ b. 2^{101}, 2^{n+2} c. 9,900, $n(n+1)$

15–1. 4,158, $n+(n+76) = 108$ $n = 16$ 16, 17, 18, ..., 92 $38 \times 107 + 92 = 4,158$

15–3. Train length: 0.1 mile   Tunnel length: 1.5 miles
90 miles per hour = 1.5 miles per minute = 0.1 miles in 4 seconds.

Do a Simulation

16–A. Answers will vary. The probability of winning a prize is 24/70 or about 0.34.

16–1. 1,800 five–digit numbers are divisible by 50.
Smallest: 10,000 = 200 × 50   Largest: 99,950 = 1,999 × 50

16–3. A, B, C → 8, 2, 4   D, E, F → 8, 8, 8

Use a Model

17–A. There are two possible surface areas.   (16 in^2 and 18 in^2)

17–1. 24 of the smaller cubes will have 2 red faces and 8 will have no red faces. Each edge of the original cube was 4 units long.

17–3. Suppose n is the largest number of feathers on any one turkey.
Number of turkeys: 1   2   3   . . . n $n+1$
Number of feathers: 1   2   3   . . . n x $x = 1$ or 2 or 3 or . . . or n

Use Dimensional Analysis

18–A. One mile = 1609.344 meters. (2.54) (12) (5280)/100 meters

18–1. 315 people were interviewed.

18–3. 6 blue cubes will balance with 5 white cubes.

Identify Subgoals

19–A. Angle ABC has measure 31.5 degrees.

19–1. Scott and Tom will be tied 1 meter from the finish line. Scott will win the race.

19–3.

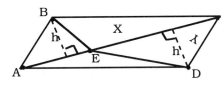

Both regions have $\overline{EC}$ as a base and both have altitude h to that base. Area (region X or Y) = 1/2 · EC · h.

Use Coordinates

20–A. 6 square units

20–1. Jane's average rate was 8 miles per hour.
Total time = $(x/2)/18 + (x/3)/8 + (x/6)/3 = x/8$
Average rate = $x/(x/8) = 8$ miles per hour

20–3. 11 trains, counting the 1 at the start and the 1 at the end.

Use Symmetry

21–A. The first player can be a sure winner. Start by placing a marker on the dot at the far left (middle dot). Then place a marker on the dot that is symmetrically opposite the one placed by your opponent, unless you can place a marker to complete a string of 3.

21–1. Each angle has measure 135 degrees. (Regular octagon)

21–3. 11 candy bars   (187 = 11 × 17   17 cents each → 32% off)

ANSWERS TO ADDITIONAL PRACTICE PROBLEMS

1. 3 inches from each edge and 3 inches between the pictures

3. The average is 9. No. The largest possible number is 106.

5. a. 1600   b. 179   c. 56   d. 2491

7. $\dfrac{5}{11}$

9. a. 4 m/sec   b. Not possible since the first lap takes 160 seconds.

11. Glen is 100 meters from the starting line in the direction Leo is running.

13. Option B is better when 11 or more vacuum cleaners are sold per month.

15. 96,312   (97,336 - 1,024 = 96.312)

17. a. 81   b. 181

19. 46

21. A B C → 16 5 4   D E F → 9 18 25

23. a. 500   b. 1000   c. 999   d. 2000

25. 82 posts

27. $\dfrac{3}{4}$ $\dfrac{19}{12}$ $\dfrac{29}{12}$ $3\dfrac{1}{4}$

29. 22

31. 400 (500 odd numbers are less than 1000. 100 have 3 as the ones digit.)

33. 74

35. Ken

37. a. 5   b. 2   c. 6   d. 7

39. Possible answers: 29:32, 29:43, 29:54, 29:65, 29:76

41. 1. 1000   2. 651   3. 400   4. T

43. 2 cm   3 cm   3 cm

45. Put 1 white ball into a box. Then put the remaining balls into the other box.

47. $2.85

49. 44

51. 22 feet by 43 feet

53. 5 (2 of same color)   13 (4 of same color)   25 (7 of same color)

55. 91

57. 31 tables

59. 10 (not married =15, not a homeowner = 20, not a car = 25, not a VCR = 30 → 100 - 90 = 10)

61. 0.16   (0.8 × 0.2 = 0.16)

63. 9

65. 14

67. 41472

69. 120 seconds

71. 56

73. 36 gallons

75. 72 minutes

77. a.

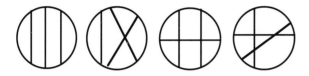

    b. 37

79. 31 grams

81. 55%

83. 211   667   In general, $n = 3x$ or $n = 3x - 1$, where $x > 1$.